KATHLEEN FERRIER

A Memoir

KATHLEEN FERRIER AT THE EDINBURGH FESTIVAL

KATHLEEN FERRIER
1912—1953

A Memoir

Edited by
NEVILLE CARDUS

with contributions by

NEVILLE CARDUS
ROY HENDERSON
GERALD MOORE
BENJAMIN BRITTEN
SIR JOHN BARBIROLLI
DR BRUNO WALTER

With 50 Illustrations

HAMISH HAMILTON
LONDON

First published in Great Britain in September 1954
by Hamish Hamilton Ltd
90 Great Russell Street, London, W.C.1
Second Impression, October 1954

*All proceeds from the sale of this book
will be devoted to the
Kathleen Ferrier Memorial Scholarship*

Printed in Great Britain by
W. S. Cowell Ltd, Butter Market, Ipswich

CONTENTS

Introduction by Neville Cardus   *page* 11

NEVILLE CARDUS
     The Girl from Blackburn   13

SIR JOHN BARBIROLLI
     Kathleen . . . The Last Years   36

BENJAMIN BRITTEN
     Three Premieres   54

ROY HENDERSON
     Per Ardua . . .   62

GERALD MOORE
     The Radiant Companion   85

DR BRUNO WALTER
     Farewell   109

The Royal Philharmonic Society's Gold Medal   115

Recordings by Kathleen Ferrier   120

LIST OF ILLUSTRATIONS

1 Kathleen Ferrier at the Edinburgh Festival   *Frontispiece*
  (*Reproduced by courtesy of 'Picture Post' Library*)   *& Jacket*

The photographs listed below will be found in two groups
Between pages 32 and 33

2 Aged one, with her mother, sister Winifred and brother
  George
  William Ferrier, Kathleen's father, photographed by herself

3 Her first Press notice
  Aged ten, with her uncle, Albert Murray

4 Aged twenty-one
  In Post Office amateur theatricals, 'The Three Knuts', aged
  seventeen
  (*Reproduced by courtesy of Turnbull, Blackpool*)

5 On her return from her first American tour in 1948
  (*Reproduced by courtesy of Associated Newspapers Ltd*)
  Aged twenty-five
  (*Reproduced by courtesy of Tassall Ltd, Carlisle*)

6 Accompanied by John Newmark in America
  (*Reproduced by courtesy of 'The Louisville Courier-Journal'*)
  With Roosevelt Williams in America, during the second
  tour

7 In Florida
  Another part of the States

8 With Benno Moiseiwitsch returning from the third American tour
In New York

9 In *The Rape of Lucretia*, with Margaret Ritchie and Anna Pollak
(*Reproduced by courtesy of Angus McBean*)

10 First recital in London, 1942
This photograph appeared on her first programme, 1942.
(*Reproduced by courtesy of Tassell Ltd, Carlisle*)

11 Between rehearsals at Glyndebourne
(*Reproduced by courtesy of 'The Times'*)
In *The Rape of Lucretia* with Flora Nielsen
(*Reproduced by courtesy of Angus McBean*)

12 The two Lucretias
With Benjamin Britten and Peter Pears
(*Reproduced by courtesy of the 'Nottingham Journal'*)

13 With Sir John Barbirolli and his mother, October 1948
(*Reproduced by courtesy of the 'Daily Mirror'*)

14 In *Orpheus* at Glyndebourne
(*Reproduced by courtesy of Angus McBean*)

15 Rehearsing with Carl Ebert at Glyndebourne
(*Reproduced by courtesy of Particam Pictures*)
As Orpheus at Glyndebourne

16 *Lieder* Recital at the Edinburgh Festival 1949, with Dr Bruno Walter
(*Reproduced by courtesy of Norward Inglis*)

17 V.I.P. in Holland
(*Reproduced by courtesy of Particam Pictures*)
With Peter Diamand in Holland
(*Reproduced by courtesy of Particam Pictures*)

Between pages 64 and 65

18 With Field Marshal Montgomery, Edouard van Beinum, and Peter Pears in Holland

Photographed in Holland
(*Reproduced by courtesy of Particam Pictures*)

19 With Benjamin Britten, Edouard van Beinum, and Peter Pears in Holland
(*Reproduced by courtesy of Particam Pictures*)

20 With Gerald Moore in Carlisle
(*Reproduced by courtesy of Tassell Ltd, Carlisle*)

21 A striking studio portrait
(*Reproduced by courtesy of Fayer*)
With Krips in Salzburg

22 On holiday in Switzerland

23 With Mr and Mrs Alec Maitland at Dundonnell

24 With Winifred Ferrier outside Notre Dame in 1951

25 In hospital on her birthday, 22 April 1951
With 'Bernie', convalescing

26 Convalescing in Cornwall and Sussex

27 Portrait by Cecil Beaton, 1951

28 C.B.E. day, 1 January 1953
(*Reproduced by courtesy of the 'Evening Standard'*)

29 *Orpheus*, Covent Garden, February 1953
(*Reproduced by courtesy of Houston Rogers*)

30 *Orpheus*, Covent Garden, 1953
(*Reproduced by courtesy of Houston Rogers*)

31 Scene from *Orpheus*, Covent Garden, February 1953
(*Reproduced by courtesy of Houston Rogers*)

32 The last photograph, taken by Douglas Glass, April 1953
(*Reproduced by courtesy of 'The Sunday Times'*)

INTRODUCTION

I t is not possible to make more than a general expression of gratitude for the many offers of help received in the making of this book. I have been deeply touched at the proofs of devotion to a great artist, a devotion shared in every part of the world.

My distinguished collaborators have made editorship easy; each of them, a master in his own medium of expression, has patiently and boldly coped with the art of writing, which, though related to our mother speech, is not immediately tractable. They have all given themselves wholeheartedly to a labour of mingled pride, sadness, happiness, regret and love.

I owe debts also to the valuable illumination and information contributed by Miss Winifred Ferrier, who is able to bring a memory of her sister to life in a few words. Mr Thomas Duerden, organist and master of choristers at Blackburn Cathedral, has provided many important details about Kathleen's formative years as a singer. Dr J. E. Hutchinson, one of her first teachers, has been enlightening concerning the crucial 'prentice years of her career. Dr Reginald Jacques has thrown light on her gifts as a Bach singer. From Amsterdam Dr Marius Flothuis has done much to fill in the Continental background of appreciation; and Miss Doris Ormerod, Headmistress of Crosshill School, Mr Justice Ormerod and Miss Claire Campbell have also come forward with details calculated to lend intimacy to our portrait.

To Mr Hamish Hamilton I am especially indebted. He has, so to say, been the book's conductor, always maintaining the ideal tempo for a publisher, never hurrying his executants along too quickly but taking care not to encourage any loitering by the way.

N.C.

LONDON
June 1954

THE GIRL FROM
BLACKBURN

by

Neville Cardus

WHEN Kathleen Ferrier was eighteen years old, in 1930, it was extremely improbable that one day she would become renowned either as a singer or as a woman beautiful to look at. She was then a raw-boned Lancashire lass. Her mother, sitting by the fireside in a homely home in Blackburn, sometimes contemplated her younger daughter carefully and said: 'Hey, but I'm ill off about our Kath. She's going to be so plain.'

Another obstacle in the way of the discovery of the truth about her gifts, stiffer to get over than any plainness of face, was the fact that already she had proved herself a pianist of unusual promise. Before her fourteenth birthday she passed the final grade of the Associated Board of the Royal Academy of Music and the Royal College of Music. She had scarcely entered her nineteenth year when she won first prize and a gold medal at a musical festival in Liverpool; the test piece was the Scherzo in E flat of Brahms. Two years earlier than this she had come in an easy winner at a 'national' piano-playing tournament held in Manchester; and one of her adjudicators was Harvey Grace, not given to the praise of misplaced talent. At another competitive festival, in Liverpool, she won first prize playing the 'Waldstein' sonata of Beethoven; the adjudicator described the performance as one that, in his opinion, 'could not have been improved upon'. His name remains a matter of conjecture. She was made L.R.A.M. in 1931.

Nearly twenty years of her life had passed now, and only another twenty remained in reserve for her, yet nobody had so far remarked upon the voice, except possibly a connoisseur or two on the telephone in Blackburn, men of acute and imaginative senses, who would risk a call any dull evening in the hope that a girl's response, rich as a plum, might be heard. She worked as a girl at the switch in the Post Office. Why was the voice, her singing voice, not found at once, before the launching of her musical talents in the pianist's direction, a diversion which might easily have deprived us of the Kathleen Ferrier we remember today? Almost by chance she swapped horses in full-flowing midstream of a career. The story is well known – how she entered another competition, now at Carlisle in 1937, and of course took first prize in the piano group. She happened to hear a singing class or bout next door. 'I think I could make nicer noises than those', she said; and a friend wagered with her, to the extent of a shilling, that she would not go into a contest for contraltos. She accepted the challenge, and was awarded the Rose Bowl, the Blue Riband of all North of England's aspiring vocalists. Years after, when she was at the height of her power and glory, she told me in reminiscence of the shilling bet at Carlisle: 'They called me K-K, Klever Kath'. She never broke away from the humour of Lancashire, loving always to play with words and alliteration, savouring them with appetite. Sooner or later, we must believe, the voice would have asserted itself; but the risk of a sidetracking to competent piano-playing was, we can realize in retrospect, alarming in a life with no time to lose. A metamorphosis of technique, of circumstance and of spirit occurred in time, just in time. And as she entered her proper territory, as song and poetry opened her mind and heart, she blossomed from girl into the warm, woman-natured Kathleen Ferrier, who ranged from Blackburn to Vienna, from gold medals in Lytham to 'Das Lied von der Erde' in Salzburg, from 'Number Engaged!' to the heartbreaking isolated tones of 'Blow the Wind Southerly'.

The early background of her musical activities was typical of a Lancashire and Blackburn not exalted by television and radio. She 'appeared' at a 'celebrity' concert in the King George's Hall on Sunday evening. The principal names on the bill-posters are of Wilfred Worden, 'the Famous Blackburn Boy Pianist of the Royal Albert Hall and London and Continental Concerts; Essie Ackland, the Celebrated Contralto; Louis Godowsky, the World-Famous Violinist of London and Continental Symphony Concerts, etc; Harold Noble, the Popular Baritone, of Leading Provincial Concerts . . .' Then follows, like an afterthought, 'Kathleen Ferrier at the piano'.

The report of this concert did its best to render justice to the young accompanist. 'Another Blackburn musician to distinguish herself', wrote the reporter, turned music critic for the occasion, 'was Miss Kathleen Ferrier. As accompanist she was not much in the limelight, of course. An accompanist's task is indeed a thankless one. Miss Ferrier', our critic continued, 'satisfied all demands, and both vocalist and violinist expressed their confidence in her, and their gratitude.'

Several years later, in 1938, she again claims the attention of the local press at a concert, but now she is a singer at a concert in Workington, in aid of the Infirmary and United Steel Companies' Old Colleagues Fund. 'She possesses a voice of magnificent range,' attested a Cumberland reporter, 'and her rendering of "Curly-headed Babby" will live in the memory of those who heard her.' Magnificent range or no range at all, we are no nearer, on the face of it, to the point in time and space at which Kathleen Ferrier and Bruno Walter will be heard and seen in conjunction on an autumn afternoon in the Usher Hall, during an Edinburgh Festival, singing and playing and getting to the heart of the matter with Schumann and Brahms.

Kathleen Ferrier was moved to decisions and ways of life very much by intuition; at any rate, she was not given to intellectual analysis or a cautious weighing-up of likelihood. It was herself who one day, two years before her capture of the Rose Bowl at Carlisle, put momentarily aside ambitions reaching towards fame as a pianist. Without a word to her closest friends she knocked at a door of a house in Preston New Road, Blackburn, where Thomas Duerden gave singing lessons. He was organist of St John's Parish Church and today he is organist and master of choristers at Blackburn Cathedral.

When he opened the door on this May afternoon and saw Kathleen, now twenty-three and her smile already capacious, he imagined that she had called just to chat or 'drop in for tea'. 'I've come to see if you'll give me lessons', she said. 'What for?' asked Duerden. 'Oh, I want to go in for the Blackpool festival!' Even then Duerden thought she was referring to piano classes; he had recently heard her mother say, 'When our Kath starts to sing I always tell her to shut up'. But he was quickly made to realize the seriousness of her present purpose. She sat down on the piano stool, after throwing her music-case on the floor. 'Precisely what is this?' said Duerden to himself, under a professional impression that part of a teacher of singers' job is himself to accompany the vocalist at the piano. But Kathleen proceeded to play to her own singing; and her song was an 'Ayre' by Thomas Bateson. 'I remember the peculiar feeling I had when she began', writes Mr Duerden in a letter dated 1 February 1954. 'Here was something rich and rare.' Her vocal range was, as early as this, from low C to high B flat, each note a tone powerful and full. She was from the start an enquiring and thrilling student to teach. 'She knew', affirms Mr Duerden, 'how a piece of music would sound without need to touch an instrument. She knew precisely which note she had to listen for in any chord. Kathleen had great natural musical gifts as well as powers of mimicry and imitation. She was extremely responsive to the demands of musical interpretation.' Best of all, she was always ready to get down to the spadework, to submit to a system of exacting exercises. She studied with Mr Duerden nearly a year, competed for the prize offered to the Tudor Class at the Blackpool Competitive Musical Festival of 1935, did not win it, but at last she had seen the light on her proper path. The journey to Mr Duerden was her own secret. Maybe the challenge unwittingly uttered by her mother made her set her strong jaw. She was never slow to show relish of a sporting chance and would not, as they say in Lancashire, be 'bested'. Not many of the world's beauteous singers have been described by their mothers as 'plain' and told to shut up. Such remarks can, of course, be made in Lancashire with implications of affection. Mrs Ferrier may actually have listened to Kathleen's voice with all a doting mother's pride. It is a Lancashire custom to lock endearment up in the heart except at weddings, Christmas, and at funerals.

Kathleen was born on 22 April 1912, in Higher Walton, near Preston. Her father was the village school-master, and he moved to Blackburn at the beginning of 1914, where Kathleen lived without scarcely ever leaving the place, on her county's borders, until she had found herself and was gallivanting to quarters as far apart and distant as Vienna and New York. Blackburn, though built on gritstone and famous for weaving and spinning, is a shade removed from the county's hinterland in social accent; they talk a 'little bit more well-off' in Blackburn than, say, in Oldham. It would not be snobbish for a Blackburn resident to point to a certain difference of atmosphere between that of his county borough and that, for instance, of Bolton. Blackburn was once a medieval Hundred known as Blackburnshire, and in 1926 became the centre of a new diocese, emanating from Manchester. The parish church became a cathedral. Robert Peel and John Morley were born not far from this parish church of Blackburn, where ninety years earlier Henry Smart had been organist at the age of eighteen. A Blackburn man's reminder to you of these facts does not mean that he is setting himself above the clogs and shawls of 'jannock' Lancashire, where one touch of nature and a goal scored by the 'Rovers' against the Arsenal makes the whole county kin. He is merely insisting on an accurate assessment of social values. So Kathleen Ferrier, though sufficiently and ripely a Lancashire lass at first sight, was different in her county flavours from, say, Gracie Fields. She did not come from the clogs and shawl environment; but, all the same, it is good to know that she remembered all her life the first pair of clogs she wore when she was a little girl. Our mind's picture of her is complete if we know that once on a time she really did go clacketty-clacketting along the Blackburn streets.

The Ferriers came from Pembrokeshire during the industrial ferments in Lancashire in the nineteenth century. Lancashire was often garrisoned by troops. From Pembrokeshire a Regiment of Foot was sent there, including Private Thomas Ferrier. He married a Lancashire girl, and a fresh branch of the Ferrier family grew from the Blackburn soil.

The Ferriers inherited from Thomas of the Regiment of Foot an enthusiasm for vocal and choral music. William, Kathleen's father, and his brother George, belonged to a

St Cecilia Society, and later William joined Dr Herman Brearley's contest choir, a body which won many prizes in northern competitive festivals. Another of Kathleen's uncles was conductor of what was then known in Lancashire as a 'weekly sing', which everybody attended for the fun of it all. In fact, several of Kathleen's relatives sang or in other ways expressed a liking for music. Her father had a rich voice with a formidable low A. He, like nearly all the singing music-lovers of the North-country, was an expert in tonic sol-fa, reading notation by aid of it. He was essential Lancashire, one of the many characters of the county, hard workers all, and not given, any of them, to wasting time. They described the ways they used their leisure as 'recreations' or 'hobbies'. Music was in those days the recreation of hundreds of Lancashire men and women, from the schoolmaster to the knocker-up. I have seen a Lancashire choirmaster at work on a rehearsal of the *Messiah*, just before Christmas. 'Listen to me,' he said, 'listen to me, you bass-siz, get yo'r chest full for "And the Government". And follow mi beat. An' another thing – never mind what you've all been hearing at 'Allé concert. It's me's conductin' thee tonight, not 'Amilton 'Arty!'

These men did not make music from an aesthetic point of view much different from the aesthetic point of view passionately held by pigeon-fanciers. They certainly did not regard music intellectually as an affair of abstract forms and patterns. They were all for the 'expressive' tone. They were always talking about 'expression', about 'drawing tone out'. And the right tone, the right expression, was one which inspired smiles and happiness in a gay song, and tears and a brimming heart in a sad one. Obviously this view of song and the interpretation of it was Kathleen Ferrier's from beginning to end.

Her mother, daughter of a mill manager, was forty years old when Kathleen was born, the father forty-five. It was through the mother's enterprise that the family moved to Blackburn, for she was determined that her three children, Winifred being Kathleen's elder sister, should receive as good an education as could be found in the vicinity. She had herself wished to become a school-teacher, but when she was eight her mother died and then, after her father had married a second time, it was made her job to stay at home and help with the house. She was a woman of sharp intelligence, unusually 'temperamental' for Lancashire, and ambitious, determined that her girls should achieve the things denied to herself. Music in some shape was taken for granted in the family, which certainly did not live under the shadow of Satanic mills; on the contrary, the dwelling-house of William Ferrier was in sight of trees and a spacious park, in which Kathleen played tennis. And for a Lancashire lass to play tennis twenty-five years ago was to be a Lancashire lass marked out from ten thousand.

From this homely world, whose music ranged from Handel and Mendelssohn to Eaton Faning, did our heroine emerge. Given a remarkable voice, nothing exceptional or marvellous would have been needed to explain why a Lancashire girl should have risen to eminence as a singer of oratorio or of devotional music and music of normal sentiment. There is no cause for wonder that Kathleen

Ferrier moved us in time with her singing in the B minor Mass, in the *Messiah*, in *Gerontius*. These are works belonging *in excelsis* to the climate that nurtured her. But how did Mahler come in? By what act of imaginative perception and metamorphosis did she in a fleeting career come to find the key to Mahler's heart and nervous system – Mahler, the composer most removed of all composers from English habits of emotion and musical experience; Mahler a neurotic, an egoist mixed in the elements, a composer who seldom smiled except ironically, Mahler the unchartered spirit who sang the swan-song of nineteenth-century romanticism in music. By what alchemy in her mind and bloodstream did a woman of Blackburn, of Lancashire goodness of heart and humour, a woman exuding from her North-country nature a loving kindness that was communal, inspiring friendship, brotherhood and sisterhood – how did she come to sing Mahler, sing his song of loneliness in the world as few Austrian singers have done, and no other English singer ever?

Obviously the legend of Saint Kate, already created, won't do. From her county and her father she assimilated and acquired warmheartedness, relish of broad fun, and a ribald joke, and a shrewd protective understanding of the price and value of everything. In her diaries and engagement books most items of her personal expenditure are scrupulously noted, day by day. For example: Shoes, £7. 7s 0d; Pyjamas, £6. 6s 0d; Taxi, 12s 6d; Train, £3. 7s 8d; Porter, 2s 0d. The Celt in her possibly counteracted sanity and proportion. Her mother was highly strung, variable in moods, at the psychological extreme to her equable husband. In Kathleen, balance of sense and sensibility was made. A general instinct for respectability, and a view of people and of the world and music eminently conformable was, I often felt, the cause of the reactions of her speech and love of laughter in the direction of the uninhibited, not to say unmentionable. She would tell a ribald tale with all the taste and refinement of a fine lady in a Restoration comedy. She could lend to a sequence of swear-words the rhythm of hexameters. 'We always had plenty of fun in our family', she would tell me. It was a family which, like Kathleen herself, mingled in proportion conventionality with impulses sometimes frustrated, to protest against, not to say play mischief with, conventionality. Her only brother, six feet eight in his stockinged feet, migrated to America. Her mother's younger brother went to Equatorial Africa, farther away from Blackburn even than Vienna. Kathleen attended the Blackburn High School for Girls and belonged for awhile to the Girl Guides, and was for a time a member of the James Street Congregational Church choir. She was plainly not unmixed in the elements; we prefer on the whole a lady or a gentleman to an artist in this country. The power and sway of Kathleen Ferrier over thousands of her own people was the consequence of the fact that she could always be at one and the same time, both.

Kathleen Ferrier's intensive training as a pianist, though it could easily have side-tracked her into a vastly overcrowded profession in which her personality might not have come to us fully and intimately, gave her a musicianship better than, and far beyond, that of most singers. Her approach to a song or any music written for the voice was never purely vocal; she conceived it and presented it as a whole – *durchkomponiert*. Her excursions into the literature of the piano, while she was very young of years and impressionable, enlarged a view locally acquired of music mainly directed towards choral virtuosity; and choral singing in Lancashire and the North of England, not forgetting Yorkshire, is often cultivated to a quite morbid perfection.

In 1924 Kathleen was judged fourth in a competitive piano class of forty-three, all under the age of thirteen; the adjudicator was Dr C. H. Moody, and the test pieces were Prelude in E minor (Bach) and 'At Eventide' (Schafer). A year later – her adjudicator was Julius Harrison – she played Debussy's 'En Bateau', and was second in a class of twenty-six with ninety marks. She was fourteen when she played at the Blackpool Festival of 1926. I have before me the adjudications of a piano competition which she entered in 1926 for piano sight test and piano solo. And the judge was none other than Granville Hill, my colleague as music critic of *The Manchester Guardian*, a first-rate pianist himself. Of the sight-test he wrote:

Reading was fairly accurate in notes in first page but it was very slow in tempo. Wrong chromatic notes in the second page at the outset, but in later parts of the section the chords, etc, were grasped more firmly.

Of the piano solo, Hill wrote:

First piece: a rather uncertain opening but playing quickly improved. The florid work had 'flow', and the phrasing was effective. In the second piece the expression was delicate and appropriate. The touch was dainty in staccato passages, but more firmness of outlines was necessary in the second page. Marks awarded, 79.

The titles of the test pieces used on this occasion are not given in the reports.

She went in for competitions at North-country festivals regularly every year, always as we have seen, as a pianist, until the wager and Rose Bowl victory at Carlisle. In 1930, significantly, she entered the open class for accompanists at Lytham; the test was the slow movement of the Mendelssohn Violin Concerto. John Wills awarded her third place; there was also a sight test with eighty-three marks. As early as in these 'teen years instinct in her was sniffing the right way of the wind – for her. She was eager to develop as an accompanist, and she here became known to two Blackburn vocalists of sturdy county fame, Annie Chadwick and Tom Barker. For the next two or three years Kathleen travelled up and down Lancashire with them as an accompanist. Both were members of the James Street Congregational Church choir in Blackburn; and Kathleen joined it too, and her first serious attempt at singing in public was in the trio 'Lift Thine eyes to the mountains' from *Elijah*. This event occurred in 1931, the year in which she gave her first broadcast, a piano recital from Manchester, her programme the Brahms Scherzo in E flat minor and 'Shepherds Hey' of Percy Grainger.

Her piano teacher was Fanny Walker, a native of Blackburn who studied with Matthay. She had a reputation throughout Lancashire as a remarkable woman, a musician of knowledge and integrity, and she was thoroughly experienced in her vocation. Amongst her pupils were counted no fewer than five hundred L.R.A.M. and A.R.C.M. diplomas. She was a teacher as much concerned about her students' quickness and accuracy of ear as about their finger technique. She was never tired of drumming into their ears a necessary caution in Lancashire, against musical festivals unless they are regarded not as goals in themselves but merely as preparations to a musical excellence to be pursued for its own sake.

With her life now before us, as we contemplate the course of it, quick to ripen after a late spring, then to blossom in a summer never to know autumn, these groping novitiate days in Blackburn and Lancashire, with competitions and 'grand' concerts, and Congregational Church *Elijahs*, and Fannie Walker and Annie Chadwick, conjure before the imagination a moving simplicity of purpose, as though of arrows earnestly shot at the nearest target to hand. I confess to having felt no slight emotion when I came upon a line in a letter of one of Kathleen's Lancashire friends: 'I have clear memories of Kathleen here, and used to tease her as she went on the platform to play. She was such a happy girl. I can see her now as she came through Lowther Gardens swinging her music-case.'

The Rose Bowl triumph at Carlisle, we might suppose, settled the issue of her future once and for all. 'I congratulate you heartily,' said Dr Staton, the adjudicator, to the twenty-five-year-old contralto, 'you have been given a lovely voice. Treat it well, and some day, perhaps, you will be a great singer.' But the singer's name at this cross-way of her life was not Ferrier – she had married and was now known and hailed by the audience as Kathleen Wilson. The marriage was dissolved – with nobody to blame. Suppose it had been immediately successful – wouldn't Kathleen, with her warm heart and her love of Lancashire life, have given herself wholly to her children and her husband, remaining content to make music in her own home? I doubt if she would have turned away from it to embark on the wandering life of a concert singer. It is a nice point. Her disappointment in marriage probably canalized her emotional impulses in the destined way; and aim and purpose were consciously or subconsciously crystallized. But in 1938 she is still entering Rose Bowl competitions, winning easily, in her twenty-seventh year, and moving to lyrical praise her adjudicator, this time none other than Maurice D'Oisley, once a lovely and stylish tenor in the Beecham Opera. 'This is a beautiful voice,' he said, 'warm and velvety. It makes me imagine I am being stroked.'

Next year, 1939, with clouds of war already heavy enough to darken the dawn of the career of a singer in ten thousand, she wins the *Cumberland News* trophy, again at Carlisle. Dr J. E. Hutchinson, one of the judges, said of her, 'There are possibilities here that are rather marvellous'. The signal fell at last, the green light showed. Kathleen put herself in Dr Hutchinson's care; he began intensively to lead her to cultivated vocalism. His task was easy enough; nothing except sheer bad luck or the misadventures of war could hold her back at this point. In fact, wartime gave her the chance, which at her time of life, at the pinch, she urgently needed. Not a long stretch of time bridges 1939 from 1953.

She made her first serious appeal to musicians when, during the war years, she was heard in Westminster Abbey in the *Messiah*, conducted by Reginald Jacques. Dr Jacques has assured me that few, if any, singers in his experience have sung Bach with the ease and accuracy note by note of Kathleen Ferrier. She never needed the usual vocal expedients. Dr Jacques did much to help her on the way to a style essentially classical. She was soon making friends everywhere by her singing and by her warmth of presence: here, on the Continent and in America. I could have filled a book with letters of tribute sent in from most parts of the world. I will quote only one of these, from an Amsterdam musician, Mr H. Flothuis:

The first impression of her voice I received in the autumn of 1946, when she sang *Lucretia* in Holland, which I heard only by radio. This was really something never heard before. In 1947 I began a composition which I dedicated to her. . . . I first heard her *in natura* in 1948. The impression of her true harmony of body, soul, and spirit deeply touched me. A thing that was noticed by many of her audience was that she mostly did not cling her hands together while singing but she simply dropped them. She was completely relaxed, and though her singing was always full of the highest tension, you could never become tired from listening.

In 1949 she was engaged for a number of performances in the Holland Festival. She had to sing in several new works, some of which she had received only shortly before coming to Holland. I had the pleasure of studying them with her. . . . She learned very quickly, except when she was tired. At that time she also sang *Orféo*. I attended rehearsals and noticed that she was loved by everyone – even by people who had nothing to do with music at all, members of the technical staff, etc. I was once waiting for a telephone call in the room of the porter of the concert. Suddenly, without any introduction, the man addressed me and said: 'What a voice, sir – and a nice woman too!'

She was a woman of high inner distinction, not perhaps of all-round spiritual education. And she knew this; once, after having sung *Das Lied von der Erde*, she said: 'I think one must be much older than I am to be able to sing this work'.

Mr Flothuis also tells of the song she promised to sing, written for her by a Dutch composer. She first saw the manuscript score a day or two before her recital, and promised to include it in her programme after reading it at sight. Flothuis asked her if he might write a translation of the words into English. 'No,' said Kathleen, 'I'll try to sing it in Dutch!' Next day she took a few lessons in pronunciation, and the day after she sang the song in the original from memory.

She was irresistible, so much so that a music critic needed a core of hard 'objective realism' not to be swayed by her personal radiance and goodness into appreciation of all that she did. It was her inner glow of nature that attracted to her a circle of constantly adulatory friends who would have ruined an artist possessing less than her powers of severe self-criticism. Everybody is a different person to different people. Sometimes when I have heard Kathleen's closest friends speak of her I have almost thought that they were discussing some other Kathleen, different in essential ways, from the one I knew. I met her not more than half a dozen times, nearly always alone. We were on terms which made it natural that whenever we met or parted she could unselfconsciously offer me her cheek to kiss. She was always happy but willing to talk seriously at my prompting. I never heard her express entire satisfaction with any performance of her own. And she was generous about other singers if they were really good. I have heard her speak of pretenders with a sarcasm equal to the best barbs of Shaw or Mr Newman. She would have been the first to let out a hoot of derision at any view or picture of her in the attitude of halo'ed and unchanging meekness and indiscriminate kindliness of heart. 'I didn't get this chin for nothing', she would say, clenching it.

When she sang at the first large-scale recital in London, in the Royal Festival Hall, I ran into the dilemma bound to come my way sooner or later. At last I was in duty obliged to write of her, finding serious fault, not with her singing but with the gestures of hand and head and the 'facial expression' (it was nothing less!) which she indulged in as though to make points in the 'Frauenliebe-und Leben' cycle of Schumann. After the concert I walked up and down the Embankment battling with my conscience. The human being in me wanted just to 'forget' everything about the concert except the beautiful singing. The critic pointed out that irrelevances and artificialities in a platform manner might easily cheapen style seriously if not stopped in time. ('Good God,' he said, 'she actually looked at her hand when she was singing "Du Ring an meinem Finger"!') A critical notice was written after a night's sleeping upon the matter; it was severe but the animadversions were toned down by language never before used in the *Manchester Guardian*, such as 'This beloved artist . . .'

But I remained unhappy, so I decided to explain in a letter to her why I had been obliged to make my criticism. She replied almost by return:

My dear Neville,

It was kind of you to write, and I appreciate it very much. I know I use my hands and I am trying to get out of what is an unconscious gesture – one must be told of these things, because it must be most irritating. I suppose it's hard to please everybody – for years I've been criticized for being a colourless, monotonous singer – 'this goitrous singer with the contralto hoot' said *The New Statesman* – so I have plodded on! I adore the 'Frauenliebe', and I can see that girl growing up from a child to a woman – and these light songs are all the highlights of joy and sorrow. If someone I adored had just proposed to me, I should be breathless with excitement and unable to keep still; and if I had a child, I should hug it till it yelled, so I can't help doing it this way, especially as I usually sing it to English audiences with little or no knowledge of German. I probably underline more than I ordinarily would the changes of mood.

But I promise you I am never aware of the audience to the extent that I do anything to impress or wake 'em up! I admit I was more nervous than usual at my first real London recital. I don't think you were 'unkind' – it's just made me to think, and that doesn't do anybody any harm.

The date of this letter is 11 November 1952.

But it was an interpretation at the extreme to those of classical or standard composers which brought her to the notice of great musicians in Europe, who might have admired with a certain reserve her methods and sincere warm-hearted demeanour in oratorio and certain kinds of song. I refer, of course, to her singing in *Das Lied von der Erde*. She was always ready gratefully to acknowledge her debt to Bruno Walter, who revealed to her the 'tone-world' of Mahler. Also, she would say, he removed those inhibitions which in English singers frequently 'keep them shy of letting themselves go'; emotionally, she meant. She would say things like this with a full Lancashire flavour. It was at a performance of *Das Lied von der Erde*, during the Edinburgh Festival of 1947, that I heard her sing for the first time. I had been told by a mutual friend to get in touch with her on my return from Australia. During this performance she could scarcely finish the last two repetitions of the word 'Ewig' at the end. She was in tears. Afterwards in the artists' room I met her and, as though she had known me a lifetime, said: 'What a fool I've made of myself. And what will Dr Walter think of me?' I told her she needn't worry, for I was certain that Bruno Walter would reply, taking both her hands in his: 'My dear child, if we had all been artists great as you we should all have wept – myself, orchestra, audience, everybody . . .'

I have known foreign lovers of music who have failed to feel a romantic poetry in her singing; maybe they have been put off the scent by an inbred North of England kindliness and generosity of temperament which do not as a rule go well with poignancy of a romantic and wounding kind. She was, as a fact, a sympathetic rather than a poignant singer. Even in Mahler, to whose secret she came as we all know close indeed, she brought with her a consoling, comforting vocal embrace which soothed the nerve of the music. Kathleen Ferrier was far removed from neuroticism; it didn't come easily to her to express a

AGED ONE, WITH
HER MOTHER,
SISTER WINIFRED
AND BROTHER
GEORGE

WILLIAM FERRIER, KATHLEEN'S FATHER
PHOTOGRAPHED BY HERSELF

PIANIST'S SUCCESS.

Fine Achievement by Blackburn Girl.

Miss Kathleen Ferrier, aged 14, daughter of Mr W. Ferrier, head master of St. Paul's School, Blackburn, has passed the final grade of the Associated Board, Royal Academy of Music, and

Jetta, Blackburn.
MISS KATHLEEN FERRIER.

Royal College of Music—an unprecedented success for so youthful a student.

She began her pianoforte studies before she was five, and passed every examination—primary, elementary, lower, and higher divisions, intermediate, advanced, and now the final—at the first attempt.

The pieces for the final grade are similar to those set for the L.R.A.M. diploma, and Miss Ferrier's achievement inspires the greatest hopes of her maturer work as a pianist. She is a pupil of Miss F. E. Walker, of Montague-street, Blackburn.

HER FIRST PRESS NOTICE

AGED TEN, WITH HER UNCLE,
ALBERT MURRAY

AGED TWENTY-ONE

IN POST OFFICE
AMATEUR
THEATRICALS,
'THE THREE KNUTS',
AGED 17

ON HER RETURN FROM
HER FIRST AMERICAN
TOUR IN 1948

AGED TWENTY-FIVE

WITH ROOSEVELT WILLIAMS IN AMERICA,
DURING THE SECOND TOUR

ACCOMPANIED BY JOHN NEWMARK
IN AMERICA

IN FLORIDA

ANOTHER PART OF THE STATES

(*Above*)
WITH
BENNO
MOISEIWITSCH
RETURNING
FROM
THE THIRD
AMERICAN
TOUR

(*Left*)
IN NEW
YORK

IN THE RAPE
OF LUCRETIA
WITH
MARGARET
RITCHIE AND
ANNA POLLAK

FIRST RECITAL IN LONDON, 1942
(THIS PHOTOGRAPH APPEARED ON HER FIRST PROGRAMME, 1942)

(*Above*) BETWEEN REHEARSALS AT GLYNDEBOURNE

(*Below*) IN *THE RAPE OF LUCRETIA* WITH FLORA NIELSEN

(Left)
THE TWO LUCRETIAS
(Below)
WITH BENJAMIN BRITTEN
AND PETER PEARS

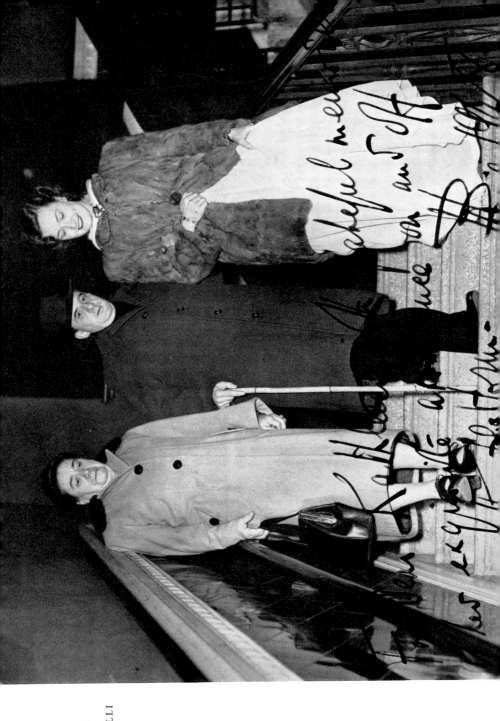

WITH
SIR JOHN
BARBIROLLI
AND HIS
MOTHER

IN *ORPHEUS* AT GLYNDEBOURNE

AS ORPHEUS AT GLYNDEBOURNE

REHEARSING WITH CARL EBERT
AT GLYNDEBOURNE

LIEDER RECITAL
AT THE
EDINBURGH
FESTIVAL, 1949,
WITH DR BRUNO
WALTER

(*Above*)
V.I.P. IN
HOLLAND

(*Left*)
WITH PETER
DIAMAND
IN HOLLAND

pathological state. Her singing, like the woman herself, was strong of spirit and imbued with a quiet but reliant sense and a feeling for the fun and goodness of life. There was no surface glamour in her art and little exhibition of sex; it is no accident that her only attempts at opera were in *Orféo* and *The Rape of Lucretia*.

We must not forget, as we count the blessing of ever having heard her sing at all, the encouragement given to her when Sir Malcolm Sargent advised her to try her fortunes in London. Through the war years her experiences in camps and factories broadened a nature already broad and friendly enough. Gradually the news got around. 'The best contralto since Muriel Foster.' A friend of mine was staying in the country resting after persistent air raids in London. One spring morning he opened his bedroom window wide and he heard such tones of happy song coming from another window as he had never heard before. It was Kathleen Ferrier at her exercises.

Comparisons with Muriel Foster are not invidious, if we consider the two singers as interpreters of the Angel's music in *The Dream of Gerontius*. Both were unforgettable in different ways. When I first heard Kathleen Ferrier singing in *Gerontius* I thought her tone and general style too reliant and rather masculine. Then I remembered that the Angel in *Gerontius* is not intended as a symbol of womanliness as the earthbound know it, not intended to represent the 'Ewigweibliche', but is a wonderful Being sent to guide and take hold of the soul of Gerontius. The mingling of an impersonal grandeur with tenderness free of sentiment made her interpretation of the Angel one of the most moving experiences, musical and spiritual, of a lifetime. After I heard her in *Gerontius* a second time, I wrote a notice praising her in lavish language. 'But', she said, afterwards, 'you didn't like me in the *Dream* last year, and I sing the music just the same now.' 'Yes,' I answered, 'but I missed the clue then. I was thinking of Muriel Foster, who was all lovely, intimate, melting, sisterly tenderness. But you, whether you know it or not, give the impression that you are really an angel.' Without a moment's hesitation, and with a smile which anybody would have loved to jump into, she replied: 'But, luv, I *am* an angel . . . !'

She was, as I think, at bottom a singer of classic dignity and seriousness. (I don't mean, of course, that she couldn't give us a lighthearted, not to say a comic, song.) The nuances of psychology and pathology of *Lieder*, especially Wolf's, were likely to elude her, though this is not to say – indeed, it goes without saying – that she could not with great appeal identify herself with Schubert, Schumann, and Brahms. The classic dignity of her art and the essentially classic 'make-up' – or *Gefühl* – of her was revealed in the almost intolerably moving and bodeful perform-ances as Orpheus (only two) which brought her career to an end, and her life, but for a few months. Seldom has Covent Garden Opera House been so beautifully solemn-ized as when Kathleen Ferrier flooded the place with tone which seemed as though classic shapes in marble were changing to melody, warm, rich-throated, but chaste. We who guessed the truth knew the physical pain she was enduring while she, unwittingly, was becoming a part of the immortality of Gluck, as far as this country is concerned. At the second performance, her last, pain visibly martyred her; and it was not Orpheus alone that sang 'Che farò' that night but all who loved this wondrous Lancashire lass.

That she was taken from us in her full rose and prime is grievous yet, nearly beyond the scope of philosophy to bear. Consolation must be sought in the fact that she lived a joyous and a full life, and during her short span emerged from a provincial obscurity to take her place in the international scene of music, where she could always feel sure that she was not only esteemed as an artist but loved everywhere by everybody. She was as brave in the face of vicissitude as she was happy in all weathers. Blow the wind southerly. She had the gift that radiates happiness. Her personal qualities even transcended her art; for great though she was as a singer, she was greater still as Kathleen Ferrier. Those of us who had the good luck and blessing to know her will never be able to separate in memory the artist in her from the warm, laughing, kind, serious, fervent, great-hearted and always uninhibitedly alive and human girl and woman that she was day in and day out, in good times or ill. Not since Ellen Terry has any artist been so universally loved.

KATHLEEN ... THE LAST
YEARS

by
Sir John Barbirolli

THERE have been certain moments in my life when I have had to face tasks of the greatest difficulty. I doubt, however, if any of them compare with the difficulty of trying to write about Katie.[1]

Why should it be so difficult? To begin with, there is the grave danger of setting down a string of superlatives when writing or talking about her which in the end would tend to become meaningless. In her character was an almost startling simplicity which leaves little scope for elaborate analysis. Her sense of humour was of the broadest, and some of her comments on people and personalities in the musical world were edged with an almost Restoration sense of imagery and directness; bowdlerized for publication they would lose all that rich and salty tang which was their essence, so perforce they have to remain the treasured possession of such of us as had the good fortune to hear her utter them.

[1] I shall always refer to her as Katie, the name Evelyn and I always called her by.

Hand in hand with this almost Rabelaisian trait in her was a sense of propriety of almost Victorian ferocity as far as her own personal behaviour was concerned.

It is possible that this great simplicity and directness of mind, fortified by a deep sense of duty and personal probity, was the foundation on which was built that sublimely heroic façade which she presented to the world when the inevitability of the final tragedy became daily more apparent. Apart from her sister Win, and the blessed Bernie who meant so much to her, I doubt if there is anyone more qualified than myself to speak of this; for during the last two years of her life a great deal of her work in this country was done with me, and, in addition, an ever-growing intimacy with Evelyn and the notorious Barbirolli 'family' brought us in almost constant contact. Of this period she would often say, 'These have been the happiest years of my life', invariably adding, 'What a lucky girl I am'. In view of what she knew of herself one cannot but marvel at this almost Olympian acceptance of her destiny.

It was when I first began to prepare a performance of *The Dream of Gerontius* in March 1948 that some of my players who had taken part in a few of her earliest broadcasts (early morning ones, with a kind of salon orchestra) came to me and begged me to have her sing the Angel. When I told her of this later she ruefully commented: 'I remember I got two guineas for the broadcast and someone charged me five quid for arranging the ruddy parts!'.

Except for ten weeks in the summer of 1942, I had been in America since 1936, and of course did not yet know of the rise of this phenomenal young singer. We were to do Elgar's *Sea Pictures* soon after, and I thought this a good opportunity to meet and hear her. Mercifully the superlatives can be dropped for a moment. Obviously not in great sympathy with these songs, she gave a competent and cold-blooded performance which greatly disappointed and even distressed me, though I admit I had been fascinated by this lovely, grave creature, who looked so sad, for she had sensed that all had not been well. Much later, when we laughingly recalled the incident, she confessed that she had been petrified at the thought of singing with me, a petrifaction which became almost panic when I flew into one of my rare rages (acoustics of the Sheffield City Hall being one of the main reasons) and threw a score at someone, which narrowly missed her. I was relieved to find that her orchestral friends had also been disappointed, but they begged me to postpone judgement till I had heard her in *Gerontius*. I heeded them, and on that memorable day when she sang her first *Gerontius* at a Hallé concert began an association that was to bring me some rare and deep musical and personal experiences. There was a kind of disembodied warmth about her singing of this wondrous music that seemed to transcend all our feelings about it; posterity must surely accord her a place of the highest honour amongst the great interpreters of this part. Though I had been completely bowled over with the depth of understanding and the logic of phrasing she had shown here, I was not convinced that this was yet the best that could be made of her voice; and I felt there were ranges of nuance and colour yet unexplored. Frankly, I became a little terrified that owing to our local conditions and traditions she might degenerate into that queer and almost bovine monstrosity so beloved of our grandfathers and grandmothers – the 'Oratorio Contralto'. I persuaded her to take up some French music, and we started with Chausson's 'Poéme de l'Amour et de la Mer'. In spite of her protests that it was too high for her, I nevertheless advertised it for performance, and she got down to hard work on it. As I had foreseen, the sensitivity of her musical nature soon became attuned to the more flowing and transparent texture of this kind of music, with a corresponding increase not only in the range of her voice but also in her resources of vocal colouring. Some time after she was giving a recital with Bruno Walter (who had not heard her recently), and I was delighted beyond words to hear him say: 'Barbirolli, what has Kathleen been doing? It is all so much freer and easier!'.

Talking of the Chausson recalls an occasion when I found it almost impossible not to break down in front of her. It was not many weeks before she left us and she was lying in her cot at the Westminster Hospital patiently enduring unspeakable agonies; she turned to me with a smile and said: 'Tita,[1] I sometimes pass the time trying to see how much I can remember of me words, and started going through the Chausson during the night, but always got stuck in the same place'. I told her I was always doing the same kind of thing, particularly in the Bach 'cello suites I had memorized as a boy. Then she began to sing to

[1] The name she always called me, and which is the Italian diminutive of Giovanni Battista.

me the opening phrases of the Chausson in a voice with all the bloom and tender ache of spring in it; the ravages of the disease were destroying her body, but, as if in some act of divine defiance, the glory that was hers remained untouched.

Her visits to the Hallé concerts were always in the nature of a joyous family reunion, as happens when some particularly beloved member of it has been away awhile. It was an intensely Lancastrian 'do', with the place literally strewn with 'luvs'.

Here, too, we have poignant and imperishable memories of *Das Lied von der Erde* and *Kindertotenlieder*, but Bruno Walter will say all there is to be said about these.

When, in December of 1950, Evelyn and I went off on an Australian tour, there was no hint of the blow that was so soon to fall. I arrived back in Manchester at the end of February 1951 far from well, the result of an attack of enteritis and, at that time, a so-far-undiagnosed appendix. I collapsed after my first rehearsal, and was told by my old friend and great Manchester surgeon Billy (W.R.) Douglas that I should have to be 'carved up'. I was not in the least perturbed at this, but greatly perturbed that I might not be able to conduct for Katie a concert performance of Gluck's *Orféo* which was due with the Hallé choir and orchestra in a fortnight's time. I had set my heart on this and had devoted a great deal of time to its preparation.

The understanding and resourceful Billy Douglas put me to bed for a few days and said that if I was a 'good boy' and obeyed instructions, he might be able to keep me going till then. Never was a patient more dutifully docile or obsequiously obedient than J.B. at that time. Every day I was 'vetted' before going to rehearsal, and all was well. The secret was well kept, and till the day of the last performance in Sheffield (for there were three altogether: Manchester, Hanley and Sheffield) only my wife, my surgeon, and the general manager of the Hallé were aware of the fact. I confessed to Katie before the performance on the Saturday that I was to enter hospital on the Monday, and it was a being of exalted generous impulse that brought to the noble music that night an impassioned utterance which will remain graven on my heart for ever. We were to drive back to Manchester that evening, where she was as usual staying with us, but first we supped at the Grand Hotel, where, with her 'Eurydice' (Ena Mitchell), Marjorie Jegge, an old Lancashire 'buddy', and Kenneth Crickmore, the general manager of the Hallé, we had one of the most hilarious parties I can remember; so my appendix, though no longer with me, remains a thing of joy for ever. Little did I dream then that but a few weeks were to pass before she was to confide to me that she, too, was about to enter hospital. One of the first things I packed in my bag on going to the private patients' home (Manchester Royal Infirmary) was a score of *Messiah*; at last the chance had come for some real leisure to study in detail and in historical perspective this wonderful work. I can never reach the chorus 'Lift up your heads' without feelings of apprehension, for I was trying to memorize it on the day of her operation, as a vain exercise in simulated calmness. One of her first outings after she left hospital was to come and hear a full rehearsal of the Verdi

Requiem which we were giving at the Royal Festival Hall. I shall never forget how lovely she looked as she sat quietly there, completely absorbed and deeply moved. At the interval I went to her immediately, a little worried lest the emotional strain be too much for her. The typically modest remark she made to me later was: 'I felt so proud when you came up to me'.

During her convalescence I was to have many a stimulating talk on various aspects of the *Messiah*, and here it was that I discovered how her enquiring musical mind never ceased seeking illumination of the works which she never took for granted, no matter how many times she had sung them. She was in particular always worrying over the problem of bringing to 'O Thou that Tellest' the easy light phrasing the music demands, while the orchestration forced her to what she called graphically enough, 'Pump it out'. It suddenly occurred to me that, of course, Handel was in no wise to blame for this touch of heaviness; for she had probably only sung the music in the Prout or Mozart version, and why not return to the original, which is for strings only? So I realized the figured bass and brought her a certain amount of vocal comfort in that piece at any rate.

Before leaving this subject I would much like to quote from a letter she sent before my first *Messiah*. She had been, of course, engaged for it, but one of her severe periods of treatment supervened, and I had to wait for her till the next performance. The gift of letter-writing was yet another of her varied accomplishments, and I think this little quotation is a charming instance of its whimsical flavour. 'I am thinking of you so much today and wishing you well for your first ever *Messiah*. I only wish I could be there to share in your triumph, as I know it is sure to be – I think Mr Handel will revolve in pride and peace tonight instead of whizzing round in bewilderment at the strange things done to his heart's outpouring!'.

While looking up this letter I came across another in which she makes illuminating reference to her feelings as to what the Chausson 'Poéme' had done for her. It was after a performance at Nottingham, about the fourth or fifth she had sung. 'I think the old Chausson is growing a bit now, isn't it! I enjoyed it really for the first time last week, and now I feel I'm getting away from a *Messiah*-like sound!'

It must have been about this time that the rebuilt Free Trade Hall was ready for its official opening by Her Majesty the Queen Mother (then Her Majesty the Queen). Knowing from past experience the intense and knowledgable musicality of Her Majesty, I wanted to make a programme that would be appropriate to the occasion and at the same time give her pleasure. In addition to Maurice Johnstone's colourful and spirited overture *Banners*, I chose the Handel-Harty *Water Music*, principally because I felt very keenly that my brilliant predecessor should be represented in some way; Vaughan Williams' *Serenade to Music*, so that the Hallé choir, and its incomparable chorus master, Herbert Bardgett, could also take its share in the proceedings; my own *Elizabethan Suite*, the suitability and significance of which I think are fairly obvious; and then came the question of the final item to make a fitting climax.

After much thought I had what proved to be a real inspiration. Since this was a great Lancastrian occasion, what could be more fitting than to have the most exquisite and resplendent Rose of Lancaster, our Katie, as soloist in Elgar's 'Land of Hope and Glory'. By some alchemy of sincerity and inborn genius, she made the rather outmoded words seem not in the least incongruous, and lifted the whole thing to a noble climax which moved everyone, not least the conductor, to tears. I don't think I can do better than to quote a writer in the *Manchester Guardian*:

And a grand climax of Miss Ferrier, the chorus, the orchestra, and a good many of the audience singing 'Land of Hope and Glory'. Here was a tribute in superb dimensions to many a great day in the old Free Trade Hall. A household tune of strong direct sentiment, wonderfully magnified. It was fine and it was right, but lovers of this tune will fear that never again can they hope to hear it in such glory. There were few dry eyes, as notices of such events used to say. And even those most heavily afflicted throats forgot during those rousing minutes to cough.

Katie was at her most radiant during the time of the reopening festivities; she stayed on, and we even managed a drive into parts of Cheshire, the cool charm of which county completely captivated her. She was particularly enchanted by the villages of Gawsworth and Prestbury, and the little black-and-white timbered church at Marton. These few extracts from a letter written immediately after she left us that week-end show, I think, how much it had meant to her to be associated with the Hallé at that time. Referring to the week-end she said:

It has been a memorable and very moving one for me, and I have never been so proud to take a small part in your concert and triumph and to see, although I know it already, the love and respect Mancunians have for you – they BETTER HAD! [in large capitals] . . . The run round Cheshire was an eye-opener and a delight on Sunday; and as for Sunday evening – what fun, what food, what *festa* . . .! It has been a memorable and most lovely few days, and I have saved some of the heather and rose petals of my posy to keep and gloat over in my old age! . . .

'What food' is a reference to some of Mémé's (the family name for my young-old mother) Festival efforts in the kitchen. From this time began a growing intimacy with my family, which I like to feel brought her much solace and quiet content.

I have said earlier that she often referred to these years as 'some of the happiest of my life'; and I want to emphasize that we, her friends, who loved her dearly, have brooded so long on the tragedy of it all that we are apt to forget this was, in a sense, really true. Quite often she would talk to me wistfully of the loneliness attaching to an artist who had reached the position she had attained in the musical world. On the one hand, the popular conception of glamour, adulation and endless entertainment; on the reverse side of the picture the constant travelling, memorizing in train, ship and plane, and the enervating, exhausting process of having to appear at your social best when body and soul cry out for peace and rest, the heart for the simple satisfactions of family life. The loss of the father she adored and had brought to London to live with her, and to whom she always very sweetly and amusingly referred to as 'Our Father which art in Hampstead', had been a severe blow, though she consoled herself with the thought that he had been spared the anxieties of her illness and operation. From this time to the end was a constant succession of periods of great activity and enforced rest and treatment; it will ever remain a physical and medical miracle that not only did she continue her career at this time but actually made an astonishing advance in her art, coming to an almost premature maturity, as if there were no time to lose. Writers and people have often speculated on what a Mozart or a Schubert would have achieved had they lived longer. Like them, Katie, I am convinced, had completely fulfilled herself as an artist, and, who knows, perhaps has even been divinely shielded from much of the harsh reality of our present-day world. It is in her flat at Frognal near the Heath she loved so well that I like to think of her best. There, with Win, and Bernie, and Evelyn, I can call on a host of happy memories; the times I used to go and cook for her, not forgetting the times she used to cook for me. She was an expert in that delectable but difficult art of fish and chips; but there was one revolting dish both she and Bernie adored which I was never, mercifully, even asked to sample. A strong, thick Scotch broth would be made, into which dumplings were introduced. So far, so good, but the climax of this – to me – extremely unsavoury culinary operation consisted of keeping back a dumpling or two well impregnated with onion and other vegetables, to be eaten with golden syrup! It is a heartening thought that even our Katie had her lapses from grace.

Apart from this one blot, however, innate taste in all things was hers; it is extraordinary how quickly this developed when she became aware of a world of lovely things denied her in her youth. It will come as a shock to many to know that she had been regarded as rather a plain child, and I must confess that I would have found this difficult to believe but for the fun we had one afternoon looking through bundles of old photographs. Although she looked a buxom, handsome lass in her early twenties, there was still no hint of the grave beauty and loveliness which were so soon to manifest itself. The dormant beauty of her art which lay within her was to bring a physical transformation on its awakening, to culminate in a radiance that memory will never dim.

She had a passion for eighteenth-century furniture and glass, and my Evelyn, who is really an authority on the latter, was in this matter guide, philosopher (when you pick a wrong 'un), and friend. She had, too, a natural palate for wines; on her last two birthdays, when I was privileged to entertain her, these were selected with loving care. For those who might be curious to know where her tastes lay, here is the list, though it is fair to point out these were the wines 'de grande occasions', not her staple diet. A Pouilly Fuissé '45, a Lafite '34, Bollinger '43; and as for port, one year it was a Taylor '27 and another a Cockburn '12. This last had been generously given me by Billy Douglas from a fast-dwindling pre-war cellar, and it was saved so that the occasion, the forty-first anniversary of the year which had produced a King of Wines and a Queen of Song, could be appropriately toasted.

It was rare for her iron self-control ever to falter, but on the occasion of the first birthday 'do', as she liked to call it, occurred a touching little episode. There were just the four of us, Katie, Bernie, Evelyn, and myself, and I had managed to get a musician-cum-baker friend to produce a rather nice cake. It was decorated with garlands and lyres and appropriate musical quotations from *Orpheus* and four candles, one for each decade. At a given moment the lights were put out; I entered with the lighted cake and she burst into tears. Smiling through them, she explained: 'Please forgive me, but, you see, this is the first birthday cake I have ever had!'

She had been our first guest when we moved into our new flat, and from now on was never allowed to go to an hotel when coming North for her engagements. She was very domesticated and happy and insistent on doing little chores about the place. We are the fortunate possessors of a treasure named 'Nelly' who comes to help daily, and I shall always have a picture of our little kitchen with Nelly washing and a glamorously dressing-gowned Katie drying. At first this so overawed our Nelly that I feared the crockery bill would show ominous increase, but she came to love it all, and it is now for her a treasured memory, like the treasured memories Katie has left for millions the world over. As Liszt in music had the gift of releasing the genius of others, so did she have the gift of releasing all that was best in those with whom she came into contact. In the summer of '52 she spent some time with us all in Sussex and fell ever more deeply in love with the county of which Hilaire Belloc, in a poem of haunting wistfulness and charm, once wrote 'She blesses us with surprise'.

She had first gone there at my suggestion in the late spring of '51, after her operation, and spent some happy weeks painting and gently exploring the country round Alfriston. This time, with the car, we took her a little farther afield, and the truth of Belloc's words became ever more manifest. How her sense of beauty was stirred at the sight of Stopham Bridge, of which E. V. Lucas had written, 'It has the beauty not only of form but of gravity; a venerable grey in a world of green'. Amberley enchanted her with its sheer Sussexness (if I may coin such a word), all thatched roofs, whitewashed cottages, and flowery gardens; and a day of delights found its perfect cadence at the 'Dog and Duck' in Bury, where, if memory serves me aright, a remarkable cricket match between the single and married women of the hamlet was played some time in the eighteenth century. Yes, she was happy then, and would regale us with anecdotes of her early days, such as her 'half-crown piano', an instrument she won in a competition for which the entrance fee was half a crown at the time she was in the local choral society. Talking of the choral society, I wish I had enough literary ability to conjure up a picture of the lingual dexterity with which she pronounced the word 'Hallelujah'. It was a sight to be seen and savoured; and she would recount with perhaps unholy glee how she used this fascinating if slightly ribald accomplishment so that her friends could see where she was to be found in the choir. There was, too, the story of her as one of the finalists at the 'Golden Voice' trials, when she became so nervous owing to the momentousness of the occasion that posterity was deprived of the joy of hearing her saying 'At the third stroke, etc' owing to the 'popping in' of an extra aspirate. How we laughed, too, when she recalled 'putting me foot well in' at the Harewood wedding. It was soon after I had received my knighthood, and she was under the impression she had greeted me as *Mr* B. The reality was much worse, or, as I prefer to think, better. A large and distinguished gathering was waiting to assemble at the top of the church steps, and as I came within sight I beheld a gorgeously-gowned and magnificent-looking Katie, who greeted me in sonorous and broad Lancashire as 'Hullo, luv!'. It made my day.

During this summer we had often talked of a project very near to my heart. I had begun conducting some opera again, and in the early autumn she came often to rehearsals, thoroughly enjoying the kind of leisure her previously intense activities had denied her. Seeing her there in the Royal Opera House at Covent Garden, it struck me as rather ludicrous that whilst we were attempting to give opera in English of the highest standards our greatest singer merely sat there listening. Also gnawing at me was the knowledge that, but for some unlikely miracle, time was short. Here I must pay unqualified tribute to David Webster, who, with infinite insight, kindness, courage, and understanding immediately agreed to put on an entirely new production of *Orpheus* in the New Year. I advisedly use the words courage and understanding; for with her final collapse after the second performance it became clear by how narrow a margin this final gift to the opera-going public was made possible.

During the next few months, a time when she had to

cancel many engagements, she found a new interest in playing 'cello sonatas with me, whenever the Hallé and Covent Garden left me a moment; and sometimes Evelyn joined us in some trios for oboe, 'cello and piano, a most attractive combination, by the way. Of course there was her painting too; and the unforgettable hours spent with her as we practically re-translated the whole of *Orféo*. Whilst my 'cello-playing, I am assured, retains some of its supposedly former distinction, my piano-playing is of the most dubious nature, but I could manage the recitatives, and I wish some young singers could have eavesdropped and learned with what infinite patience and degree of self-criticism her great results were obtained. Another thing which made work with her so absorbing and rewarding was though I might make her repeat a phrase *ad nauseam*, there was never a hint of impatience or resentment if she knew that what we were both searching for was right. At Christmas she sang her last *Messiah* with us at Belle Vue, before a vast audience of six thousand. It was difficult at the time to realize that this was to be so; for she was in fine fettle, not only vocally (though, as I mentioned earlier, it was extraordinary how her voice remained completely unaffected throughout this period), but physically too she seemed better. Movement which had become on occasion more difficult seemed freer, and that night, Evelyn having an important broadcast in London, she acted as hostess for me at a little dinner party I had for some particularly close friends of hers who had come for the performance. The Maitlands from Edinburgh, Ben Ormerod (Mr Justice Ormerod, who had played the tympani in the Blackburn Orchestra when she sang her first *Messiah* there), and Billy and Meg Douglas. The artist who had earlier in the day moved us all to tears by her nobly poignant utterance of 'He was despised' ended the evening by convulsing us with a supremely professional performance of a very naughty cabaret song.

May I recall just one more family remembrance before we pass on to the final triumph and tragedy. I was 'in the know' about her C.B.E., and I thought it would be nice to announce it at midnight on the 31st to the assembled Barbirollis (there are eleven of us at full muster), on this occasion reinforced by Win and Bernie. A New Year's Eve 'do' was accordingly arranged, and at twelve o'clock we toasted the new Companion.

Soon after began that saga of fortitude and courage that inspired us all during the final weeks of preparation for *Orpheus*. These rehearsals brought her much happiness, though she was already then beginning to suffer greatly, and movement was becoming difficult. Here her sense of humour shone at its resplendent best, and I shall never forget the impish glee with which she literally purred over one of the critic's comments that her movements were an object lesson even to the Sadler's Wells Ballet. The searing beauty of the only two performances which Destiny granted her I will not dwell on; they remain an imperishable memory to all who heard them. These were to prove her farewell to us as an artist; and no artist ever said farewell with greater eloquence or dignity. As those of us near to her said on that memorable night in February, when at the close of the performance people threw their own flowers to her from the auditorium, 'She was perfect to the end'. Those of us who had the sombre privilege of being near to her in her last days can repeat, 'She was perfect to the end'.

And so, beloved Katie, can I take my leave of you with these, I think, not oft-quoted words:

> 'Not without honour my days ran,
> Nor yet without a boast shall end,
> For I was Shakespeare's countryman
> And were you not my friend.'

THREE PREMIERES

by

Benjamin Britten

IT WAS in the last days of the war, at a performance of *The Messiah* in Westminster Abbey, that I first heard Kathleen Ferrier sing. I was impressed immediately by the nobility and beauty of her presence, and by the warmth and deep range of her voice. It seemed to me (and seems so still) that hers was one of the very few voices that could tackle with success the low *tessitura* of that alto part. So, a few months later, in the autumn of 1945, when we were looking for a contralto to play the name part in a new opera I was writing, *The Rape of Lucretia*, and she was mentioned as a possibility, I enthusiastically welcomed the idea. Peter Pears, singing with her a few days later, suggested it to her, and she tentatively agreed. She was nervous about learning a new long, modern part; nervous, above all, about her acting – I think she had never been on the stage, certainly not the professional stage, in her life. She was persuaded, especially since the rehearsal period was going to be long and calm, and soon she was keenly involved, greedily absorbing each new bit of the score as it came along, and helping in the arrangements too; it was she, for instance, who suggested Nancy Evans to play the other Lucretia (we were preparing a 'run' of the opera, and so two alternating casts were necessary). Thus in no time her warm friendliness and keenness on any serious artistic matter made her a member of the 'family' which was planning this operatic venture. The 'family' consisted of such as Ronald Duncan, who was writing the libretto of the opera; John Piper, designing the scenery and costumes; Eric Crozier, producing; Joan Cross and Peter Pears singing, with Kathleen, the principal parts; and myself writing the music.

As the rehearsals progressed during June 1946, at John Christie's little opera house at Glyndebourne in Sussex, Kathleen's diffidence as an actress began to disappear – not entirely, as she was easily crushed by a cutting remark. Vocally she was always secure, although the violent hysterics and the short transition to the long, soft line of the 'Flower Song' in the last scene of all had to be 'managed', and to be studied carefully under the devoted guidance of the conductor, Ernest Ansermet. I think we were all aware that a star was rising among us, although no one could have behaved less like a star than Kathleen did; in fact, her close friendship and friendly rivalry with the other Lucretia (Nancy Evans), remains one of the happiest memories of that time.

She was naturally nervous on the first night (12 July), and in the interval, in spite of the great beauty of her personality and her lovely singing, the act was considered to have gone to the male and female chorus. But at the end, her nobility and the deep pathos of her 'confession' brought Lucretia, the tragic Roman matron, right to the fore.

Many performances of the work were given that summer and autumn: two weeks (if I remember rightly) in Glyndebourne, then a tour of the provinces, with a week each in Manchester, Liverpool, Edinburgh, Glasgow and Oxford, and a season of two weeks back in London at Sadler's Wells Theatre. All this time Kathleen's Lucretia grew steadily in stature, always vocally richer, and her acting slowly more relaxed, until it became one of the most memorable of contemporary opera creations. She was always least happy about the 'hysterics' I mentioned before, partly because it was the least close to her own nature, and the part was in *tessitura* very high for her. One note at the climax, a top A, was quite out of her reach, so I wrote her an *ossia* of an F sharp. At one of the last performances at Glyndebourne, listening from the side of the stage, I was startled to hear her let out a ringing top A. Afterwards she confessed that she had got excited, forgotten her caution, and the F sharp, and was equally startled to hear herself singing an A (the first she had ever sung in public, I think I remember her saying). After that it was always the A, and I crossed F sharp out of the score.

The season ended with a visit to Holland, with performances in Amsterdam, and The Hague. It was her first visit abroad and she enjoyed it all hugely. Everything fascinated her – the people, the food and drink (the Dutch gin!), the remarkable countryside, also some of the sanitary arrangements. She managed to project a stream of hot water from the hand-shower through the window of her bathroom into the street below. After this visit, in which she made such a deep impression, she was frequently to return to Holland. She eventually had almost as many friends in that country as in England, and her death caused widespread distress there.

In the summer of 1947 she again repeated her beautiful performance with us at Glyndebourne, but after that her concentration on oratorio and *Lieder* made her less available for opera. But she kept her affection for the part, and when, for the English Opera Group season at the Lyric, Hammersmith, in the Festival year, 1951, we asked her to play Lucretia again for us, she happily agreed. Alas, a few weeks before the season was due to start she had to have the first of the tragic series of operations, so Nancy Evans took over the part.

.   .   .   .   .   .

During 1948, at the invitation of Serge Koussevitsky, I was writing a large-scale work for voices and orchestra; this was the Spring Symphony, and it was commissioned to have its first performance at the Tanglewood Festival in New England the next summer. It was the first big non-operatic work I had written for many years. Therefore, since I was so keen to hear it and I could not go to the U.S.A. for the performance, Koussevitsky generously let it first be performed in Europe a few weeks earlier, on 9 July, at the Holland Festival. There were three solo parts – soprano, contralto, and tenor – and I had Kathleen very much in mind when I wrote the long, serious setting of a poem by W. H. Auden, which is the central piece of the work. Her beautiful dark voice and serious mien, together with her impeccable intonation, made a great impression in this sombre movement. Also memorable in this most wonderful of first performances (played superbly by the Concertgebouw Orchestra under Van Beinum) was her gaiety in the trio of birds in 'Spring, the sweet Spring', along with Jo Vincent and Peter Pears.

.   .   .   .   .   .

The third and last close artistic association I had with Kathleen Ferrier was perhaps the loveliest of all, a kind of Indian summer. It was in the early days of 1952, the period after her first serious operation, and when we dared to hope that the miracle had happened, that she might possibly be getting well. It was a series of concerts organized for the funds of the English Opera Group – which, after all, she helped to launch by her wonderful Lucretia performances in 1946 and 1947 – to be given in London and the provinces by her, Peter Pears, and myself. It was a programme which we all could enjoy: early English songs, including some of Morley's canzonets, ravishingly sung, some big Schubert *Lieder*, some folk-songs, grave and gay, ending up with the comic duet 'The Deaf Woman's Courtship', which Kathleen sang in a feeble, cracked voice, the perfect reply to Peter's magisterial roar. A masterpiece of humour, which had the audience rocking, but never broke the style of the rest of the concert.

To complete the programme I wrote a Canticle for the three of us, a setting of a part of one of the Chester Miracle plays – *Abraham and Isaac*. It was principally a dialogue for contralto (the boy) and tenor (the father), although on occasions the voices joined together to sing the words of God, and there was a little *Envoi* in canon.

We performed this programme in Nottingham, Birmingham, Manchester, Bristol, and Liverpool, a broadcast, and at the Victoria & Albert Museum in London, the happiest of concerts. Everything seemed to go well, with big friendly audiences. *Abraham and Isaac*, when performed with such sincerity and charm, pleased the public. Only in Nottingham was there a cloud, but we did not realize the size of it. Kathleen seemed to trip and slightly wrench her back walking off the platform and she was in pain for some of the time. It turned out to be a recurrence of her terrible illness, but no one suspected anything – or perhaps she did and said nothing.

We all determined to repeat the concerts the next year, to write a companion piece to *Abraham and Isaac,* but operations and long and painful convalescences intervened and we had to give them up. But there was one more performance of the Canticle. Kathleen spent some days in Aldeburgh in June 1952, while the Festival was going on. She was convalescing but managed to go to quite a few concerts, lectures, and operas. Each morning my sister would walk along to the Wentworth Hotel, where she was staying, would go through the programmes with her, and she would make her choice for the day. She became a familiar and much-loved figure in the town. Finally, towards the end of the week, she joined Peter and me in our yearly recital in a touching performance of *Abraham and Isaac*. Many people have said they will never forget the occasion: the beautiful church, her beauty and incredible courage, and the wonderful characterization of her performance, including every changing emotion of the boy Isaac – the boyish nonchalance of the walk up to the fatal hill, his bewilderment, his sudden terror, his touching resignation to his fate – the simplicity of the Envoi, but, above all, combining with the other voice, the remote and ethereal sounds as 'God speaketh'. In the short run-through before the concert Kathleen failed to make her entry in one passage. Apologizing and laughing, she said she was fascinated by Peter's skill in eliding an 'l' and an 'm' in a perfect *legato* – 'Farewell, my dear son'. She really must practise that, she said, she never could do it as well.

One of our most determined plans was to make a long-playing record of this programme. Several dates were fixed at the studio, but each one had to be cancelled because of new developments of her illness. Finally, the engineers inspected her bedroom – acoustically possible, they said. So we planned to go along one evening to record the Morley canzonets, the wonderful dialogue *Corydon and Mopsa* of Purcell, which we had all loved doing, the folk-songs, and *Abraham and Isaac*. This time it seemed that there could be no hitch; although bedridden, her voice had lost nothing; the record was even announced. But another operation, the last, intervened, and in a few months Kathleen was dead.

There seemed to be one more chance, even so, of perpetuating what was for me one of her most delightful performances. We had made a broadcast of this concert, and this had been recorded and repeated several times.

Could this not be issued commercially? It seemed it could, with one or two permissions to be obtained (and eagerly granted), and the receipts would go to the Kathleen Ferrier Cancer Fund. But there was another 'but'. At the very last minute it was discovered that the recording had been destroyed 'in the course of events'. Not overmuch imagination here; for quite a time it had been common knowledge how ill Kathleen was, and everything she did had a more than usual significance. Of course, there are many beautiful performances of hers recorded for our delight, but it is my own special selfish grief that none of my own music is among them – music that she sang with her own inimitable warmth, simplicity, and devoted care, as indeed she sang everything – as if it were the most important in the world.

PER ARDUA...

by

Roy Henderson

'Oh, by the way, you will be singing with a young contralto called Kathleen Ferrier on Wednesday, and I would like to know what you think of her. I think she is quite promising.' That was the first time I had heard the name. Long experience and a shrewd judgement had given John Tillett, the concert agent, a flair for spotting an unknown artist who was likely to make a success if all went well. He lived to see the fulfilment of his highest hopes.

The concert was at Runcorn on 23 December 1942, and the work performed was Mendelssohn's *Elijah*. I was not greatly impressed by her performance. Kathleen told me a year or two later that she had been overawed and frightened lest anything should go wrong. As a consequence, she kept her eyes glued for the most part to her score, and sang with no thought for interpretation. She was 'playing safe'. There was something out of the ordinary about the basic quality of her voice. Although it was too sombre, there was a musical flow in her singing which was most pleasing. After the concert I took her aside and, according to Kathleen, said: 'Very good, my dear, but you must learn your work.'

On the following day, Christmas Eve, we travelled to London together with a soprano we met on the platform at Crewe, a great meeting-place for concert artists. Kathleen told us of her new home in Hampstead, that she hoped she would get enough engagements to stay permanently in London and that at any rate it was worth a try. We wished her luck and I saw no more of her for a few weeks.

At that time I was teaching, between concert engagements, at the Royal Academy of Music. One of my pupils told me he had been singing with Kathleen, that she was downstairs in the canteen and would like to see me. He was a very persuasive young man. Some years later Kathleen told me he had rushed her into a decision when she wanted more time to look around and take advice about a teacher in London.

'Please may I have some lessons?' These words of Kathleen's began a relationship which was to last until the tragic end. I became 'My Prof', the words with which she introduced me to anyone I met for the first time. Over a period of nine years we worked together in the studio intensively until 1947, and later when the opportunity and necessity arose. We travelled thousands of miles together, and, as a fellow artist who was also her teacher, I cannot describe the thrill of watching her amazing development. When I first met her, her name was in small letters on the programme. One day, I cannot remember exactly in which year it was, some fumbling secretary of a choral society handed me Kathleen's cheque by mistake. It took me a moment or two to get over the shock when I found that the pupil's fee was greater than the teacher's; although it continued to rise higher and higher, her attitude as a pupil never changed, though the teacher became more suggestive and less dictatorial with the passing years. We had one further and, to me, no less exciting musical relationship, as conductor and soloist, when Kathleen sang on so many occasions for my choirs at Nottingham and Bournemouth.

At the beginning of her first lesson I asked her to sing something of her own choice. She selected Schubert's *Erl King* in an English translation, as at that time she had not sung in German. I felt at once that here was a voice with which I would have to tread warily. It was so naturally good. Dr Hutchinson, of Newcastle-on-Tyne, had been her previous teacher and had instilled in her a feeling for music, a horror of any sound which was in any way tight or gripped, an easy-flowing tone, and a tongue which kept out of the way at the back of her throat. She had learnt to relax. It was a splendid basis on which to develop.

Of course, there were limitations. After two years teaching, development can only be in a very early stage. The quality of the voice was rich, but rather too dark, and it possessed but one colour. The range was only moderate; the high E tended to sharpen in pitch and lost much of the quality of the lower notes, while F was about the upper limit and was only supported by extra push of breath. The interpretative side of singing hardly existed.

It takes about seven years to make a singer, provided the material is there, and Kathleen proved no exception. The fact that she became the greatest of our time was due

(*Above*)
WITH FIELD
MARSHAL
MONTGOMERY,
EDOUARD VAN
BEINUM AND
PETER PEARS
IN HOLLAND

(*Left*)
PHOTO-
GRAPHED IN
HOLLAND

WITH BENJAMIN BRITTEN, EDOUARD VAN BEINUM AND PETER PEARS IN HOLLAND

WITH GERALD MOORE IN CARLISLE

WITH KRIPS IN SALZBURG

A STRIKING STUDIO PORTRAIT BY FAYER

ON HOLIDAY IN SWITZERLAND

WITH MR.
AND MRS. ALEC
MAITLAND
AT
DUNDONNELL

WITH WINIFRED FERRIER OUTSIDE NOTRE DAME IN 1951

IN HOSPITAL
ON HER
BIRTHDAY,
22 APRIL 1951

WITH 'BERNIE',
CONVALESCING

CONVALESCING
IN CORNWALL
AND SUSSEX

PORTRAIT BY CECIL BEATON, 1951

C.B.E. DAY, I JANUARY 1953

ORPHEUS, COVENT GARDEN, FEBRUARY 1953

ORPHEUS, COVENT GARDEN, 1953

SCENE
FROM
ORPHEUS,
COVENT
GARDEN,
FEBRUARY
1953

THE LAST PHOTOGRAPH, TAKEN BY DOUGLAS GLASS,
APRIL 1953

not to the teaching but to herself. The same teaching can be given to a hundred different people, but the final result is never the same. The teacher's responsibility is great. There are many winding lanes which appear to lead to the heights; some lead to a bog from which the pupil never rises, some to a bewildering maze from which there is no escape; some are in the right direction. The teacher can equip the pupil and point the way as it seems best to him. He may even demonstrate how to do this or that; but the foot-slogging is done by the hard work of the pupil, who needs infinite patience, determination and grit, with eyes ever on an unreachable goal.

There are four chief ingredients which flavour the success of a singer: voice, musicianship, ability to interpret, and personality. Let us take the instrument first, and see how it applied to Kathleen Ferrier.

I never saw Kathleen's vocal chords nor, to my knowledge, did any specialist before her final illness. She had a remarkably healthy throat, which she never coddled and seldom subjected to gargles and sprays. She took reasonable precautions in cold night air after some hours in a stuffy concert hall, and as far as possible kept her feet dry. To the end she knew little about the mechanism of the voice. In any examination on the anatomy of the throat she would have failed miserably. I saw no point in trying to enlighten her, as I feel it is totally unnecessary to good singing. The less conscious the singer is of the larynx the better. I advised her to read no books whatever about the voice or voice production but as many as she could on music, musical biography, and the interpretation of songs.

E

The first thing we had to tackle was the further development of her breathing. It is not my purpose to be technical, as this book is primarily for those who loved a great singer, but a little explanation is necessary. Breathing for singing is not like taking a deep breath when you escape from Town and catch your first glimpse of the sea as you get out of your car. It involves a great deal of muscular movement and control besides expansion of lung. No singer can ever strengthen these muscles or increase the expansive power of the lungs too much.

There are two methods of breathing, both of which I had tried myself. I prefer the method which is out of favour here but is much practised on the Continent. It took Kathleen about three weeks to make the change. It leads to great muscular development and is the breathing whereby Caruso was able to move a grand piano with the strength of the outward kick of his diaphragm. To develop this muscle and keep it supple there were exercises. In one of them Kathleen would lean with her back against a wall, kicking hard against the force of my fist, which I would press against her diaphragm. Many readers will remember Grace Moore in the film *One Night of Love*, where she lay on her back on the floor with books piled high on her diaphragm. She was singing while pressing outwards with her diaphragm against the weight of the books. We used the same technique without the books, by which means, together with some exercises, Kathleen became exceedingly strong and was able to sing without exhaustion those long phrases in Bach's 'Have mercy, Lord' with a magnificent grandeur and fullness of tone.

Members of the choirs sitting behind her have remarked on her great expanse of lung at the back and sides; to the audience it was scarcely noticeable.

The vocal chords or lips do not determine the warmth, beauty, or resonance of the voice, though their size has much to do with the category to which a voice belongs. Very much in the same way that one automatically changes the note when whistling a tune, so the vocal lips, which are not chords in the accepted sense of the word, set up vibrating columns of air according to the note we require. Just as some people can whistle higher and lower than others, so the range of the singer varies. The chief difference is that the whistle made by the lips is a complete sound; the sound made by the vocal chords, were it possible to detach the head, would be a squeak with no relationship to the note intended, rather like the reed of an oboe or the mouthpiece of a trumpet detached from the main instrument. It is the head, from the top of the larynx upwards, the shape and size of its cavities, its bone structure, and the direction in which this vibrating column of air set up by the vocal chords is sent, that make a voice beautiful to listen to or otherwise.

Kathleen was born with a wonderful cavity at the back of the throat. In the course of my teaching I have looked into hundreds of throats, but with the exception of a coloured bass with a rich voice, I have seen nothing to equal it. Dr Hutchinson had seen to it that her tongue kept flat on singing AH; and after I encouraged her to open her mouth more when singing full voice, one could have shot a fair-sized apple right to the back of her throat without obstruction. This space gave her that depth and roundness of tone which were distinctive. The voice rolled out because there was nothing to stop it. With so many singers one has to open up the back of the throat before any start can be made at all, often a long and tedious process; tongues and soft palates get so close to each other that the voice is bottled up or thin in quality. With Kathleen the space and the consequent warm spacious tone were there already when she sang in her first lessons.

Space is not enough. The direction in which the singer emits the breath is all-important. By altering the focus point of the blow a different quality is obtained. There must be something for this jet of air to hit against like a jet of water hitting against a wall. If it hits against the frontal top teeth the resultant sound is hard; if it hits against the soft palate with a wide-open throat it tends to bleat and lacks resonance; if it is of no fixed abode it alters the quality with every change of shape which different vowels demand, and the result is an uneven voice. I will go no further, because I am treading on controversial ground. I once spent a wet day in the Watson Library in Manchester skimming through as many books as I could on how to produce the voice. I came out by that same door wherein I went, bewildered by all the opposing theories that were supposed to be the panacea for every ill. Voice production cannot be learnt from books. What suits one person may be entirely wrong for another. In the process of making a cure, complications are apt to arise which necessitate a change of medicine, and only the teacher on the spot, if he knows his job, can himself, or sometimes with the aid of a specialist in voice production, alter the treatment accordingly.

Kathleen had a long jawbone, which no doubt gave her a set determination in all that she did and perhaps came from the famous pirate Henry Morgan, from whom she claimed ancestry. Although it gave her a magnificent full mouth, the distance from the mask of her face to the back of her pharynx made it difficult for her to produce her voice forward enough. The tone was too dark and the diction lacked crispness. Whatever we did to remedy this would have to be done carefully and slowly. Here already was a sound, the basic quality of which must in no way be spoilt.

Kathleen thrived on the vowel sound EE. This is not everybody's medicine; one must remember that she already had an open throat. We placed it to give a brighter sound without losing any of the basic beauty of the tone, and all other vowels were trained to match it. Later we got bolder and Kathleen made some queer noises to get the focus in the right place before singing songs. Her attack likewise was too far back, and we had to practise a good deal to get the start of a sentence which began with a vowel sound placed satisfactorily. In her last performances of *Orpheus* at Covent Garden she sang a florid aria at the end of Act I, which had been omitted in the Glyndebourne production of the same work. After the first night, when I went to the dressing-room to congratulate her on a truly great performance, she asked if her *coloratura* was all right. She told me with glee that she had all the words of the translation altered so that the vocal runs were on the sound EE, on which she had practised so assiduously years ago. It felt like old times and took away all the nervous terrors of a most difficult aria on a first night.

At an early lesson Kathleen brought Arthur Somervell's arrangement of Handel's 'Come to me soothing sleep', transposed down a tone, like others of her songs in those days. I wanted her to sing the word 'me' on the high D flat in the second phrase very softly. It is approached from the low E flat on the word 'to', an awkward jump of a seventh. In order to sing the note at all she had to put some weight on it. In one place later in the song she found it impossible to start a phrase on a high D flat without hitting at the note. Her attack had to be brought more forward to the point where it could be held by poise. If you stand upright you are poised. If someone is there to hold you, you may lean backwards without falling, but if that support is withdrawn, you will fall. That was exactly what was happening to Kathleen's voice. She had to give more and more breath support in order to sing higher, otherwise the note collapsed.

She worked hard at her exercises and each few months marked an improvement. The process was gradual, because she had to earn her living at the same time, and was involved in learning a great deal of music and the interpretation of many choral works new to her. One can almost sketch the development of her voice by her recordings, although they started later than the time of which I am now writing. Her voice gradually went higher, and eventually became capable of the lightest touch at the top of her extended range. Her last lessons in

voice production – one might call them road repairs –
were in 1951.

To have the best vocal technique a girl should begin in
the teens if possible. Kathleen started ten years too late,
and was further handicapped by being unable to set apart
even one year in which to devote her whole time to the
mastery of her instrument. In the end, by her natural
ability and much hard work, she played on her voice as
she willed.

What sort of a musician was she? At one time a singer
could reach the very top class with very little knowledge
of music, and the old tag which separated singers and
musicians was for the most part justified. Nowadays the
modern composer has set some dreadful problems. In
many cases they have demonstrated their total ignorance
of the capabilities of the human voice and written music
which, if it is to be performed at all, is more suitable for
an orchestral instrument. The most difficult of contemporary works Kathleen had to sing were Britten's *Lucretia* and
The Enchantress of Arthur Bliss, both written for her. As
she was able to pick and choose, she was spared any music
which was not singable. She could play the piano, and the
learning of notes presented no difficulty, another hurdle
which stops many an artist promising in other ways.
When I first knew her she already had a feeling for music
and a critical outlook on her own performance. Her
rhythmic sense was good, but she was apt to be late on
to the vowel if preceded by a consonant. The fault lay in
the opening and shutting of her jaw, which was too slow.
She soon put this right by speeding up the movement.

Her phrasing was governed to some extent by her inability to do just what she wanted with her voice; but the more she gained control of her instrument, the more she enjoyed the fascination of weaving phrases, and we would try them this way and that before deciding on the exact curve to be adopted. Beautiful phrasing became second nature to her in later years; one of the great charms to musicians was the delicacy of touch with which she could manœuvre a voice of such nobility.

As a choral conductor myself and a singer who had experienced the idiosyncrasies of beat of nearly all the conductors for whom Kathleen was singing, I was able to anticipate for her most of the tempos and snags that would await her at rehearsals. So-and-so beats out every empty bar and gives you no latitude whatever; So-and-so will follow if you take a lead. This one beats 6 here, that one takes it in 2. Do exactly as this one tells you and don't argue; So-and-so doesn't know the first thing about conducting, and it is up to you and the leader to keep it going; and so on. With an accompanist to help, I would conduct while Kathleen sang, so that she could get used to a beat, and find out what she could and what she could not do. Sometimes for fun I would try to imitate the beat she might expect from certain conductors – keep far away from So-and-so, his arm is long and he uses it with latitude. I am sure that conductors who wanted their own way, provided it made sense, had no trouble with Kathleen at rehearsal, while many a lame dog limped through a performance the easier because she was at his right hand.

One well-known conductor wrote to me after her

death to say what a privilege it had been to conduct with her as soloist. Even in the early days one had a feeling of complete confidence in all that she did. In all the concerts she sang for me, and they were many, I cannot remember a wrong entry or the slightest musical hitch. Occasionally she would want some latitude, 'to get me breath'. 'Don't forget, Prof, give me time to swallow after "Him".' This was in the middle of 'O rest in the Lord', where she usually collected more saliva than she could comfortably cope with. When she became world famous I cannot describe the thrill she gave the ordinary choral conductor like myself; after a great performance that was unforgettable her first words would be of thanks, and the inevitable question which followed every concert of hers at which I was present, 'Was it all right, Prof?'

Sometimes she would come across a conductor who ruined a performance through ignorance or pigheadedness. I would hear all about it when next we met. It might have been on the golf-course at Hendon where we were members. She would pull out her driver and say, 'I'm just going to think of So-and-so, the old basket, and give it a jolly good slosh', and away would go the ball a full two hundred yards, to her intense satisfaction. When she had been under the baton of the best conductors she became intolerant of bad performances. Latterly she was able to choose what she wanted and performed only those works with those conductors she liked, the two most beloved of whom are contributors to this book.

Kathleen always enjoyed giving recitals. The singer's dynamic range can be anything between *sotto voce* and the loudest tone possible; the music can range from most of the world for the best part of four hundred years, one can cover the whole sphere of emotions and situations, all in one evening's recital. What scope for an artist! The recital has the further advantage of adequate rehearsal. Orchestral rehearsals are costly, and the solitary rehearsal which most choral societies were able to afford for her was never much more than a run through. Amazing feats were performed, and Kathleen loved the choirs who had devoted so much of their spare time to making music. The recital, however, gave the opportunity of *ensemble*, which two musicians with less limited rehearsal can more readily achieve. In Scotland in the early days she enjoyed working with Ailie Cullen of Glasgow; in England with Phyllis Spurr, with whom also she rehearsed most of the music she had to sing. Many accompanists will claim the honour of having played for her, but her greatest thrill came from her recitals with Bruno Walter and Gerald Moore. She never debased herself by singing trash. She was a true musician.

The third quality of the singer is interpretative ability, which deals with the words of the poet as seen through the eyes of the composer. In this field Schubert's *Erl King,* which she sang at her first lesson, and Mendelssohn's *Elijah,* in which I had just heard her, were quite unimpressive. Her only thoughts were on herself, that she should do nothing wrong and make as pleasing a sound as possible with a steady flow of tone. Dr Hutchinson had very properly concentrated on first things first. Interpretation rests on vocal technique and musicianship. If we think of a building, breathing and breath control are the foundations; vocal technique is the structure, the bricks and mortar in which we want no cracks or uneven surfaces; musicianship is the elevation and the shape of the rooms, which must be artistic; interpretation includes all the fun of decoration and colour. Interpretation without vocal technique can tear the voice to pieces, without musicianship it can ruin the greatest works of art.

My first concern was that this rare organ should not suffer in any way through dramatization. Kathleen was not yet ready for Schubert's *Erl King*. We began to look for songs and choral works which suited her voice and style. Just as people differ, so singers vary in type. The great artist of experience can turn herself into several characters, like Ruth Draper, whom I advised Kathleen to see when next she came to London. Later they became firm friends. The singing voice, however, is far more delicately balanced than the speaking voice; unless the singer has very good command of the instrument it is easily displaced and damaged.

We chose Bach, Handel, Brahms, and music that required good singing without too much emotional disturbance. Verdi she would never sing. When Kathleen was on the way to world fame and was much tempted by the offer of a performance of Verdi's *Requiem* at the Scala Theatre, Milan, she took my very emphatic advice and refused it. Later when she jokingly said to Bruno Walter that I bullied her and stopped her from singing Verdi's *Requiem*, he entirely agreed it was not for her. It needs a voice of harder texture.

In the early days John Tillett often rang me up to ask if I thought Kathleen could sing such and such a work. Much depended on the *tessitura*. Her top notes needed attention before she could undertake any Elgar. Young singers so often make the mistake of trying to do everything; and I know it is not always financially possible to turn down work. But most societies respect the artist who declines a work because it is unsuitable, and are ready to engage him at the next opportunity.

It seems strange to those of us who remember Kathleen at the height of her career to realize that she was too timid and frightened of making a fool of herself to attempt anything in the way of facial expression, or go beyond the bounds of absolute decorum in emotional display.

To get rid of self-consciousness I tried to turn her thoughts to the things about which she was singing. She had a vivid imagination but had never used it on the concert platform. We painted pictures conjured up by the song. Everything had its relative position on an imaginary canvas before her. Here would be a tree in full bloom, about which she was singing; lambs playing over there; a stream running away in the distance yonder. In 'Immer Leiser' of Brahms the window was to the left and the door through which she longed for her lover to come took the chief position in the centre. It was to this door that she leaned forward in the poignant appeal of the song's last words, 'Komme bald!'.

Imagination had to go further than merely seeing things that weren't there. Kathleen learnt to hear and to feel. She heard the fury of the storm in 'Die Junge Nonne', the sad song of the nightingale in 'Der Tod, das ist die Kühle nacht'. She felt the cooling breeze on her hot cheeks as she sang about it in 'Suleika', the icy shivering wind in 'Vergebliches Ständchen'. I watched her closely all the time. If she sang the words but failed to use her imagination and see, hear, or feel, we would try the passage again and again. It was exacting work, but in the end she painted pictures which the audience could visualize as vividly as John Coates had painted them a generation before her time.

Although imagination is a help to memorizing words, it involves as much singing without the aid of a copy as possible. If one's eyes are constantly referring to a book, the picture is lost in crotchets, quavers and printers' ink. Kathleen soon found that she was inundated with work to learn. She had been used to playing for herself, which is not conducive to memorizing. One must get away from the piano, and that is why the non-pianist usually has the better memory, though his knowledge of the score is not so comprehensive.

Occasionally memory played tricks with Kathleen, as it has with all of us. Once when singing Handel's 'Where'er you walk' her mind had gone blank, and instead of 'all things flourish, where'er you turn your eyes' she had blurted out 'where'er they eat the grass'. It was all she could think of. Singing this nonsense once is bad enough but it is repeated twice, by which time her face was the colour of a beetroot.

Her first *Dream of Gerontius* was to be in Leeds in November 1944, and I particularly wanted her to sing it from memory. By this time I knew the impact she made on an audience, though less than a year previously she had been turned down by the B.B.C. at an audition for the 1944 Promenade Concerts, at which she became such a firm favourite the following years.

We spent hours and hours over the work. Every move, change of mood or expression, together with the curve of every phrase, the thought behind each sentence, the exact weight to give the key words, the facial expression, and a hundred other things, were worked out, so that it appealed not only to the ear but to the heart, the mind, the soul, and the eye. I wanted her to make this work her own.

I confess she moved me so much in our final lessons that I looked forward with the keenest anticipation to the concert, which I was able to attend as a member of the audience. At the morning rehearsal the suggestion was made, not by the conductor (Sir Edward Bairstow), that it would be much wiser for her to have her copy, as she would be likely to forget her words in her first performance. She immediately sang some wrong words, which of course in rehearsal mattered very little, but it upset her and at lunch she told me she felt she ought to have her copy. The thought that a mere suggestion, however well meant, might undo all the hard work we had put in together was too much for me. When singers, even those of experience, have a copy between them and the audience, they cannot help looking at it. Each look spoils the picture and snaps the thread of imagination between the artist and the audience. The character is lost for a moment. Kathleen knew the work thoroughly, so I did the only thing possible. I confiscated her copy, more or less with her consent, so that she went to the hall without one. At the performance not a word, not a semiquaver, was out of place, and the audience was electrified.

A good interpreter must also be a good actor. It is far more difficult on the concert platform than in opera, where one has the advantage of scenery, costume and make-up, gesture and movement from place to place. The concert singer, almost rooted to the spot, may make only the most sparing use of hands and arms, and has to represent many characters in the same evening dress, very often in cramped surroundings, with the movements of an orchestra and conductor as a further distraction to the creation of atmosphere. Even so, much can be done by facial expression and movement legitimate to the concert platform.

As much for practice as anything else, we tried out Parry's 'Love is a bable', in which there is a change of facial expression in almost every line.

'Love's fair in cradle, foul in fable
'Tis either too cold or too hot'

has four different expressions. Kathleen copied the expressions I suggested one at a time, in front of a mirror, so that she could see what she was doing. She was an excellent mimic. Sometimes it was necessary to say 'A face like So-and-so's', and at once Kathleen got it. Eventually 'Love is a bable' became one of her favourite English songs. Her face could reveal to the audience the inmost feelings of her heart, from gaiety to grief, love to hate, serenity to her unforgettable impersonations of an orang-utang.

What are the legitimate movements of the concert platform? It would take a whole book to do justice to this part of interpretation; and then an hour or two of practice is of more value. The prerequisite of movement is to learn to stand still. The stance itself is important.

If the singer stands with feet together, no backward or forward lean of the body is possible without protrusion in the wrong places. This is only possible if the feet are apart, one in front of the other. If the right foot is in front it points roughly at an angle of ten degrees to the right of a centre line, while the left foot is twelve to fifteen inches behind at an angle of twenty to twenty-five degrees from the centre line. This was Kathleen's stance, and with it she was able to transfer the weight to either foot. I encouraged her to stand with her hands by her side as well as occasionally together. During the whole of *The Dream of Gerontius* she had her hands by the side, and raised them holding them in front, with the palms slightly upwards only at the end, when singing 'Softly and gently'. For songs which implied repose, worship and anguish the hands were together, for songs of action or dignity the arms were by the side.

The position of rest has the balance of the body evenly distributed on both feet. Emotional disturbance can have the effect of altering the balance; for instance, fear will make one recoil, and the weight is moved to the back foot while the shoulder may come forward protectively. Appeal will have the opposite effect. The command 'go', if said on even balance, is unemotional. On the forward balance it assumes a threatening attitude, and with the weight on the back foot it denotes authority. The body is uplifted in aspiration and great happiness, it droops in sorrow, shame and depression, and so on.

Some songs require no movement at all, indeed the more still the singer stands the better. Others depend a good deal on the right movement at the right time. Wrong timing can make nonsense of the movement. When we studied the 'Four Serious Songs' of Brahms in 1944 we spent a great deal of time on how to look, where to look, where to move, and also the exact timings of the moves. How effectively Kathleen moved from the backward balance in 'O Death how bitter art thou' to the forward appeal of 'O Death how welcome art thou'. Although we had practised it many times in the studio, it always brought a lump to my throat when she sang it. The secret was not only in the movement itself; it was in the sincerity of her feeling, without which all singing and acting is an empty shell.

Few people realize that what appears spontaneous action is often the result of study and much practice. The movements which Kathleen made on the concert platform were not haphazard. They were carefully planned in the first instance and repeated over and over again, in the same way that a pianist will spend an hour practising one phrase to ensure the beauty of its curve in performance. Every art has its own technique, and Kathleen had to learn the craft before the artist in her rose to conceal the hard work of the studio. Every song was taken to pieces, studied and practised, often phrase by phrase. Gradually a style was mastered, and such was Kathleen's greatness that she could sing 'Die Junge Nonne', 'Bobby Shaftoe', 'Das Lied von der Erde' and 'I have a bonnet trimmed with blue' with equal sincerity and sure success. She had the great confidence of knowing that nothing had been left to chance and that every move she made looked right and enhanced her singing.

She was strong alike in tragedy and comedy. When I took her to sing to Professor Ebert, the Glyndebourne producer, on his return after the war, he was captivated and at once earmarked *Orpheus* for her as soon as it could be included in the repertoire. Meanwhile he thought she might make a sensational Carmen. Kathleen felt she could not act the part. I thought she could, but was worried about the high *tessitura* and the possibility of vocal strain, and thus for different reasons we decided against it.

It always annoyed me when the lighting of a hall was so dim that the audience could not see the expression on Kathleen's face. Once when we were giving a joint recital in a famous North-country concert hall, I asked for more light, but none was forthcoming. Eventually we sang in the only place where the audience could see us, behind the piano. I remember a magnificent performance of 'Frauenliebe und Leben' in an even more famous hall that was lost visually to all but the front rows. Kathleen was always so much better to see and hear in a hall than to listen to over the air.

Was it her voice, her musicianship and interpretative powers that brought her fame? In themselves they were great achievements, partly through endowment, partly through sheer hard work, but the crowning glory was her personality. This was herself. Even personality grew with the years and experience of life.

When Kathleen came to London she was unsophisticated and almost *gauche*. Her walk had a suspicion of hobble-dehoy about it. We practised platform deportment and behaviour, how to walk on and off, bowing, sitting down, standing up, acknowledging the help or otherwise of an accompanist. As time passed and experience grew, and her appearances were greeted ever more enthusiastically, her own warm personality radiated through her platform manner, and audiences were charmed before she sang a single note. In early years her platform appearance was greatly enhanced by her sister Winifred, who worked wonders during the difficult period of clothes coupons. I was present at the cutting out of a dress in which Kathleen can be said to have made her name. It was made by Winifred out of curtain material.

During her career Kathleen had help from many who were eager for her success. First her old teacher, Dr Hutchinson, whom she never forgot, and Hans Oppenheim, to whom I sent her when she was preparing her first *Lieder* recital with Bruno Walter. He gave her the authority of a one-time German national of great musical sensitivity. After he had taught her the pronunciation and musical style which gave her confidence, we worked together on the songs in our usual way. It was the first of many happy visits. Kathleen had not sung previously in the French language, but when she was called upon to do so for Sir John Barbirolli she had a few lessons from Pierre Bernac, which she thoroughly enjoyed. Bruno Walter, of course, taught her all the Mahler she knew, and more than anyone else helped her to world fame.

Kathleen was constantly learning from other artists. I know from my own experience that no one can give recitals with Gerald Moore without invaluable musical enlightenment and inspiration, or rub shoulders with eminent conductors and musicians of all kinds without gaining knowledge. Many gave her sound advice, chief among whom were her agents, Mr and Mrs John Tillett.

Her career was fantastic. As one who was privileged to be her teacher, I know the answer. No teaching, no musical associations, no help from whatever distinguished quarter could have worked this miracle. It was Kathleen herself, her great gift of voice, her hard work, artistry, sincerity, personality and, above all, her character that made her great.

I often wonder what happened when the last brave notes faded in the concert of her life, and the trumpets on the other side resounded with a welcome more tumultuous than any applause she had known. Did she turn to look round on her friends and the world to which she had given so generously, and as the shades of Bach, Handel, Gluck, Schubert, Brahms, Mahler and Elgar rose to greet one who had served them faithfully, did some nearby spirit catch the faintly whispered words, 'Was it all right?'.

THE RADIANT COMPANION

by

Gerald Moore

WHAT a wonderful recital it had been! There was a throng of people round Kathleen dying to touch her hand, to feel a glance from her. I stood, when I had a moment to myself, and looked at this beautiful woman. (Strange how often one gazed at Kath as if seeing her for the first time.) Yes, it had been a colossal success; the great Concertgebouw had never been so packed for a song recital before. Kathleen had had to thread her way through the crush of people down the long stairs in full view of the auditorium: a three-minute procession each time she approached or left the stage. The acclamation when she first emerged that evening would have unnerved an artist with three times her experience. And did she open her programme, it might be asked, with something easy, something light, or a song calling for a minimum of technical control? No. Her first song was Bach's 'Bist du bei mir', whose long phrases need the most constant, the smoothest stream of sound. Its slow movement and tranquillity make any short-comings of the singer flagrantly apparent. Nervousness unsteadies the breathing; this not only affects the intonation but ruins Bach's long and lovely line, here the very essence of the music. Yet she had sung it not only with ease but with a most moving tenderness; not only with a disdain for technical problems but as if poetic considerations were all that mattered. What was the explanation of this amazing control of Kathleen's? Surely the answer is that she was a born performer. Many artists are heard at their best during rehearsal and admit themselves that they are less good, through sheer fright, at performance. With Kathleen it worked the other way. She was inspired by the occasion, and the bigger the occasion the better she sang. She seemed to embrace the audience as she saw it; her nostrils dilated with excitement, her eyes sparkled with joy. As a finely-trained thoroughbred dances with zestful pride at the feel of the springing turf beneath him, so Kathleen responded to the inspiration of an audience.

Watching Kathleen in the artists' room, I began to wonder if her admirers would ever go. She ought to be feeling tired after such a strenuous evening, and longing to relax. Then suddenly she threw me a quick glance. I was waiting for this message, it was an unmistakable call for help. I pushed my way through, draped her cloak round her shoulders and, regardless of anyone, said with emphasis: 'Your car is waiting, Kathleen. I think you ought to be going or you will catch a chill.'

At last alone with her, the floor of the car littered with her flowers, we drove back to the hotel. 'You turned down several invitations for us this evening', I said. 'One from the Burgomaster. What do you propose to do during the next hour and a half?'

'I have a little surprise for you. We're going to have supper with old friends.' So, having seen to her bouquets and changed her gown, Kathleen walked out of the hotel, round the corner into a quiet street, and came to a delightful little restaurant where we sometimes lunched as a change from our rather grand hotel. I said: 'Your idea of supper here is not wanting in originality, nor is it devoid of charm. I see only one impediment.' 'And that?' she asked. 'The restaurant is closed.' 'Not to me, luv.' She tapped on the door and in a twinkling the restaurateur was there and bowing us in. 'Didn't I tell you we were going to see an old friend, Gerald?' And a sumptuous supper it was, with the *patron* and his wife as hosts.

That was Kathleen! As we four sat round the table laughing and talking, I felt how lucky we were not to be standing in a crush of people at some official reception.

This, I think, is a good example of the utter simplicity of this great woman. Holland was at her feet; the recital at the Concertgebouw was the grand climax, setting the seal on her success. And in the moment of victory she chose to be 'with old friends'.

It still surprises me when I reflect on the friends that surrounded Kath; not their number so much as their infinite variety. A woman of such renown and personal magnetism is a natural target for bores and hangers-on. The fringe of the musical world is embellished with these fluttering moths and butterflies. Anyone in Kath's position finds that these pests have such nuisance value that they retard progress like the barnacles on a ship; they mercilessly encroach on leisure, on essential and precious leisure.

If I were to say that Kathleen chose most carefully those whom she admitted to her circle of friends, it might imply that she was snobbish or difficult. That would be nonsense. The qualities that she herself possessed – warmheartedness, sincerity and simplicity – were what she looked for in others. She never told me this, for she would be quite unaware of her own attributes, yet it can safely be said that nobody could hope to be a friend of hers who was tinged in the slightest degree with meanness, deceit, or affectation. She had an instinct for making the *right* person her friend, it mattered not whether he were a dustman or a duke. Heart certainly came before brain; and yet you would not be so frequently in her company, for all your disposition, if you were not interesting. For Kath was a good listener. She who could contribute so much to a conversation seemed to delight in passing the ball to others, seemed always to try to throw the limelight on the other person. I have been in a room with twenty or thirty distinguished people and seen some of them working hard, elbowing their way vigorously to the front, in order to draw the eyes of the company to themselves. Kath never did this. She was quite content to say nothing. She shone without trying. She shone without thinking, and, despite the adulation, the fêting, the flowers, was blissfully unaware of it.

I was once in a large *salon*, one of a large assembly where the chatter was noisy, the champagne circulating. Suddenly there was silence and in strode Sir Winston (then Mr) Churchill. Was it an accident that a hush fell over the guests when he strode purposefully and unsmilingly into the room? Was it accidental that each time he addressed himself to his neighbour nobody else wanted to speak? Perhaps this is what is known as personality – or personal magnetism. In a lifetime spent amongst celebrated people I can recall few who possessed this magic: Paderewski had it certainly; you felt his presence even before you saw him. Could one say Chaliapine had this magic glow? This is open to doubt. Certainly he was a great man and a great personality, but his gigantic stature, his magnificent presence drew attention unto him rather than any deep or spiritual force. Kathleen Ferrier had the magic. When she was silent, you who were one of a crowd instinctively sought her endorsement of your opinion; your eyes sought hers. But when she spoke – you wanted to listen.

First of all her voice!

Of all the millions the world over who have heard her sing in public or on record or broadcasting, only a small, a very small percentage have heard her speaking voice. It was vibrant; it was soft and low – but always soft. Lionel Hale wrote: 'One Sunday morning, three years ago, I was sitting at breakfast with a friend in a Sussex hotel, and we were talking, as one does at breakfast-time on Sunday, about disillusion. "It is wrong", I said, "to know too much. For instance, there is a woman talking at the table behind me. Her speaking voice is enchanting: one could listen to it for ever. I don't wish to see this lady, for I'm sure her looks would spoil it!" My friend glanced over my shoulder briefly and replied: "You are wrong about the looks, but right about the voice. It's Kathleen Ferrier! Such a voice!" ' (I cannot resist dotting Mr Hale's I's and crossing his T's. The scene was Alfriston. I know, because it was there we visited her and Bernie Hammond, her dear companion, friend, and secretary.)

When she spoke you wanted to listen because she had something to say, you did not listen merely to hear a beautiful voice. She was a woman of decided opinions, but the opinions were not thrust on you; you asked for them. In a discussion or argument everybody gave their views, but you waited for Kathleen's, which were always wise without being magisterial, definite without being dogmatic.

To say that Kathleen never said an unkind word would not be accurate. Anybody with her wit and humour has a well-stocked armoury. But her barbs were light, and did not wound deeply. They were well aimed, and were always fired from the front, never behind the victim's back. Her directness could be quite startling sometimes: 'Miss Ferrier, you refused my invitation to supper at my home after your last recital here, you cannot put me off this evening.' 'I am sorry, but I prefer to return to my hotel and retire early.' 'But, Miss Ferrier, I am the President of this Society! Does that make no difference at all?' 'No difference at all.' 'This means you will never visit me!' 'I suppose it does.' This was certainly the direct treatment. It transpired that on her first concert in a certain Continental town Kathleen and her accompanist, Phyllis Spurr, after an all-day journey and a strenuous concert, had visited this same official, and no sooner had he imprisoned them in his music-room than they were regaled by piece after piece of piano music and two-piano music. 'And when you are tired out, luv, two pianos are twice as bad as one!'

Kathleen's directness saved a good deal of time, trouble' and frustrated fury. At one concert a man, a complete stranger, pushed his way through the people in the artists, room, went up to Kath and said: 'Miss Ferrier, I wanted to come round to tell you that it is a pity you included Schubert's *Erlkönig* in your programme this evening; it is a hateful song and I detest it.' Kathleen, gazing at him very much as an indulgent mother would regard a spoiled child, said very gently, 'And –?' Something in her expression made this man buckle at the knees, he said, 'And? Oh! And – er – and – nothing!' That was the end of him so far as we were concerned. I have more than once heard Kath administer a rebuff quite simply in that manner. It was not done with ostentation but with modesty and quietness.

This modesty was one of her most endearing traits. For surely it would have turned the head of a lesser mortal to have conquered the heights as Kathleen did in so short a spell. She had the balance and sense to stand up to overwhelming success and sudden fame, to the blaze of publicity accompanying one whose name is news. Proof of this was provided by the attitude of her contemporaries towards her. Musicians in the public eye for years before Kathleen was known at all felt no envy of this star who shot up like a rocket: instead they displayed an extraordinary warmth of feeling for her. English artists took a pride in the girl whose fame, internationally, had outstripped theirs at a bound; those from Spain, France, Italy,

Germany, positively enjoyed enthusing over her. (An Italian singer, whose range was the same as Kathleen's, and consequently to be considered a rival, told me that although 'Ferrier had only sung the Bach B minor Mass in Rome once, the public are still talking with wonder at the memory of it'.) I mention these things because competition in our profession is keen and, regrettably, sometimes bitter. Jealousy and spite exist here as elsewhere. Had Kathleen been only a marvellous singer these colleagues would have expressed admiration but no more. What is the explanation of the positive affection she inspired in them? The answer I would suggest is her modesty. Bernie, her companion, told me of an incident which epitomizes this. She and Kath were landing at some airport abroad and saw a reception committee waiting on the tarmac bearing bouquets and other evidence of welcome for some incoming traveller. 'Look at all the kerfuffle,' said Kathleen, 'there must be someone of importance on board.' She looked round the plane as it drew to a standstill and decided it must be a portly individual whom she pointed out to Bernie. 'Probably a statesman or some industrial nabob.' It had never occurred to her that all the 'kerfuffle' as she called it was for herself.

·   ·   ·   ·   ·   ·

Kathleen's circle of friends was comprised, as I have said, of persons of infinite variety and parts. I must mention a few of them.

One of her greatest friends was Ruth Draper.

In the spring of 1953, when Kath was to return home

after a long sojourn in hospital, it was considered quite impracticable for her to live at her old flat at Frognal near Hampstead Heath; where there were over fifty steps to climb to her front door, and no lift. In Kath's condition these steps were more than a menace; they were for her more or less unsurmountable. A charming house was found for her in St John's Wood. It had a garden. Miss Draper, who did so much to make the first Ferrier tour of America such an enjoyable one, now conceived a most delectable 'house-warming' present: she had the garden beautifully laid out and arranged for a gardener to tend it regularly for Kathleen's enjoyment.

And then there was Dame Myra Hess, who loved to accompany Kath in private, for the sheer joy of it; she lent her one of her very own pianos 'to keep as long as Kathleen wishes'.

Few people outside our profession realize the endless correspondence involved in connection with an artist's public engagements: arguments over the building of programmes, arrangement and juggling of dates, travelling details such as tickets, passport visas, hotel accommodation, and so forth. Seemingly details, they are major pre-occupations to the person concerned. Mrs Emmie Tillett performed miracles to smooth out such problems arising from the Ferrier concerts. It was she with Kathleen, sister Winifred, and Bernie who took up painting with en-thusiasm. The four of them formed what they called very grandly 'The Elm Tree Road Group'. They felt, most wisely, that it would be soothing to nerves tautened by the strain of concert work.

Kathleen loved to paint. She had read *Painting as a Pastime* – the author's name is not unknown – and it inspired her to take it up as a hobby. Two of her dearest friends, Mr and Mrs Alexander Maitland, were infected by her enthusiasm and followed her example. It pleased Kathleen enormously that they should do so, for they had long been connoisseurs. In their home in Edinburgh, where she spent so many happy times, you can see Renoir, Van Gogh, Degas, Gauguin, and the works of other masters, and you can also see the *opus* (Opus 1) of Kathleen. This is signed 'K.K.', meaning 'Klever Kaff'. I am inclined to think that it is as highly prized by the Maitlands as any other picture in their collection, even though it would never be hung 'on the line' at the Royal Academy.

John Barbirolli, on his lightning visits to London, always found time to run up to the Hampstead flat, often with his wife Evelyn Rothwell, and there they would play trios, Sir John on his 'cello, Evelyn with her oboe, with Kathleen as pianist. Their audience numbered three: Winnie, Bernie, and Rosie. Rosie was the cat.

Some of Kath's most joyous evenings were spent with her dear Hamish (Jamie) and Yvonne Hamilton. Of all of us Jamie was the most selflessly devoted. It was at Yvonne Hamilton's home that history was made: for there Kathleen met for the first time Dr Bruno Walter and sang to him.

On Bruno Walter it is hardly necessary for me to expatiate, for the inspiration she derived from his guidance is known to us all. But it is good to remember the affection and thoughtfulness this great man showed for her. On one of her American visits, when he was in New York, Dr Walter arranged for his house in California to be put at Kathleen's disposal, so that she could indulge in a complete rest for two weeks during the course of a strenuous concert tour.

Then from Cumberland there was Ena Mitchell, the soprano whose success Kath did so much to foster. Here I cannot resist relating an episode typical of Kath's thought for others. Ena Mitchell's son was in London, and he visited the Frognal flat one morning in great excitement to tell Kathleen he had been given a permanent post in one of our finest orchestras. 'You must telephone Carlisle and tell your mother', said Kath. 'Yes, I shall do that this evening, when the long-distance charges are reduced.' 'You go at once and use my telephone. Would you deprive your mother of six hours of happiness?'

And mention of the North brings also to mind the Hon. Mr Justice and Lady Ormerod and their son John. The Ormerods and 'Katie' took the greatest pride in one another, since they all hailed from Blackburn. I shall not easily forget the sweet and moving way that Sir Benjamin spoke when he proposed Kathleen's health at a little party given to celebrate her being honoured with the C.B.E. Then there was that doyen of our profession Norman Allin, whom Kath loved dearly, and Mrs Allin; and, of course, the Roy Hendersons, who, with Mrs Tillett, were her friends from the earliest days in London.

In mentioning these few I seem to neglect the thousand other loving friends she had. It is quite impossible to enumerate them all, but perhaps I have given in a vague way some idea of this absorbingly interesting circle. It was certainly heterogeneous. 'Any man', I was told by one of her friends, 'who does not acknowledge that Kathleen Ferrier is the most wonderful woman in the world, has something wrong with him.' It was not a case, let me add, of a hundred men and a girl, for though we men loved her, our wives loved her themselves.

The word 'love' has been used over and over again in my last few paragraphs, but there is no substitute. Where Kathleen was concerned lukewarm feelings did not exist. She was surrounded by the love that her personality and her gifts deserved. Our attention and our anxiety to relieve her of any strain were redoubled when we knew the nature of the illness which held her in its grip during the last two years. This, alas, was the very period when a group of young women formed a cabal against this noble woman. At first they were admirers of the great singer. They presented themselves in artists' rooms all over the country – even journeying so far as Dublin – wherever Kathleen appeared, and made a determined effort to establish themselves as intimates with her. But everyone, even a servant of the public, as Sir Henry Irving often alluded to himself, has the right to choose his own friends, and although Kathleen was always charming and patient with this little clique, she would not allow it to progress from 'fanship' to friendship. And then retaliation, or rather revenge, obsessed the minds of those who fancied themselves snubbed: anonymous telephone calls were made in the middle of the night; spiteful jokes were carefully planned. On one occasion Kathleen, who always had a car from the same hire service, emerged from her flat to sing at the Royal Albert Hall and found six cars from six different hire services waiting outside her door, all having to be dismissed by her, all grumbling at her, all demanding payment. A splendid trick to play on an artist before an important appearance! Again, returning late at night after a recital in Highgate, and accompanied home by Winifred, Bernie, Enid and me, Kathleen found that a barrage of dustbins moved from the adjoining flats, about twelve in all, had been piled one on top of the other before her front door. They were full and heavy. What would have happened had Kathleen been alone? Fortunately, we knew the identity, although we could not definitely prove it, of the leader of this gang of squalid nuisances; Kathleen's solicitor interviewed her, and was given a promise that these disgusting practical jokes would not be continued.

It was typical of Kath's sweet patience that we were far more angry about all this than she was herself.

Many tributes have been paid to the memory of this great singer. In one of them I read that tears were never far away from her. I would prefer to say that laughter was never far away, for I have never seen her weeping or tearful. I do not believe I have ever laughed with anybody so much as I have laughed with Kathleen. I still can gurgle with amusement over some of our adventures together. When we were touring, Kathleen, who was physically strong and vigorous, loved to take long walks. Visitors to Holland know how many cyclists there are in that country; and it is an ever-recurring miracle how any of them manage to live to a ripe old age, for taxis, trams, and cars seem to miss them by a hair's-breadth hundreds of times a day. Their motto seems to be 'We prefer to die in the saddle' or 'While there is life we pedal'. At all events Kath and I were the downfall of a cyclist one winter's day when we were on one of Kath's 'exercises'. We were walking in a park and heard a bell being tinkled behind us. The path was narrow. We sprang on either side, leaving precious little room on the frozen ground for the bicyclist to squeeze between us. His wheels skidded, and in the twinkling of an eye the rider was thrown, plumped down in a sitting position on the ice. The bicycle, however, righted itself miraculously, and, finding itself relieved of its accustomed burden, pursued its course merrily like a riderless horse in a steeplechase. With profuse apologies we picked up the dishevelled jockey, recaptured his steed, and off they went none the worse. And then I caught Kathleen's eye: with one accord we rushed knee-deep in snow into the bushes, so that the poor man would not hear us, and howled with laughter. Ridiculously childish, no doubt, but a happy memory now.

Another time in Amsterdam, with a good six inches of snow on the ground, Kathleen strode out of the hotel: we went on for miles, myself protesting every five minutes. At last I complained that we were getting lost; no, she knew exactly where we were. On and on we went, until she said, with a shamefaced smile, 'Ask this man, luv, the way back to our hotel'. 'Much better', I grumbled, 'if we first ask the way to Amsterdam!'

I was sitting with her in a plane once, just before the take-off, feeling a little subdued as one generally is when leaving home for a month. Suddenly we became aware that the passengers were being addressed by the steward: 'Passengers are warned to keep their safety belts fastened throughout the flight until otherwise advised, as the trip is likely to be bumpy. . . . Thank you!' An elderly lady plucked his sleeve and nervously asked him: 'Is it going to be very bumpy?' The steward turned on her and said with crushing dignity: 'Madam, I said bumpy, not *very* bumpy . . . Thank you!' I felt the seat next to mine shaking. It was Kathleen, convulsed with laughter. She made me repeat this duologue, with the slightly adenoidal voice of the one and the quavering tones of the other, over and over again until I was word perfect.

But what unselfishness! She had been the one to recognize the humour in this situation and yet she did not claim proprietory rights in the telling of the story, she much preferred to be a listener, to be able to join in the laughter if you had told the story well.

As I said earlier, Kath was happy if she could throw the limelight on others; she did this to me at a certain recital of hers in the provinces. At the end of a programme it was one of her special pleasures to sing different folk-song arrangements like 'The Spanish Lady', 'My Boy Willie', 'The Keel Row', 'Bobby Shaftoe', and so on, but at this concert I particularly remember 'The Keel Row' because I more or less improvised the accompaniment as I went along: Kathleen had no idea what I should do next, nor, for that matter, had I. It was fun doing this, and I greatly enjoyed it. It would be about the third verse that I became involved and quite absorbed in a most intricate syncopated rhythmical pattern. No doubt my false accents or un-conventional harmonies proved too much for the singer, for Kathleen started to giggle as she sang, then she turned round and the sight of my seriously concentrated face so tickled her that she stopped singing altogether, threw her head back and, accompanied vociferously by the audience, burst into hearty laughter. Through the noise I called out to Kath, 'What's the matter?'. She raised me to my feet to make me take a bow, beaming with pride as much as to say 'What a clever child!', but what she actually did say as I resumed my seat was, 'Now, luv, play it properly!'.

Although Kath was quick to detect a *double entendre*, and, as Neville Cardus suggests, would not have been the complete person she was had her humour been strictly confined to the decorous, she could clown magnificently. To hear her singing to her own accompaniment (she had absolute command of the keyboard, executing arpeggios, rapid scale passages, roulades, octaves, with an ease that made a hard-practising pianist envious), caricaturing a high soprano performing 'Sing, joyous bird!' or 'Will o' the wisp' was something that one would willingly have paid to hear in a cabaret: the whoops, the scoops, the archness, the fixed relentless smile were there unerringly, and all sung just that agonizing quarter of a tone off pitch!

Kath's facility on the piano, in my opinion, gave her an enormous advantage. It meant, when studying a new work, that she could sit down and play intelligibly the accompaniment to some song or the piano score of an opera, oratorio or orchestral work. She was a very good sight-reader. Many singers learning something new to them will be forced to pick out their own vocal line with one finger on the piano keys, but they will know nothing of the accompaniment or orchestral part till they hear it in rehearsal, when they may have to make considerable readjustment. I do not say this disparagingly or sarcastically. The fine singer of today is a first-class musician, and must be if he is to cope with the enormous range of music he is commissioned to master. His task is an outsize one, and it is just as unreasonable to expect him to be able to play the piano as it is to expect the pianist to sing.

Why, then, with these great advantages was her repertoire not even more extensive than it was? This question has often been put to me, and the answer is simple.

In the first place, and never to be forgotten, she had, to all intents and purposes, only given herself wholly to singing in the last decade of her life. It is staggering to survey the ground she covered in this spell, not only in German, French, Italian and English song but in opera, oratorio, and in such poems for voice and orchestra as Mahler's *Das Lied von der Erde* and Brahms' Alto Rhapsody.

Secondly, she was never satisfied with herself but practised, practised and practised with painstaking thoroughness the works with which one would have said she was most intimate. Everything was committed to memory. She may have been seen on the platform with a score, but I cannot remember her using one. Certainly never in recital did she carry one note of music in her hand.

With no singer did I find myself more intimately at one than when accompanying Kathleen Ferrier. It is obviously very necessary for the accompanist to arrive at a complete understanding with his partner if a perfect *ensemble* is to be achieved. In a long career in association with all sorts and varieties of singers and instrumentalists I have frequently failed to find this *rapport*. But it is consoling to remember some thrilling moments – all too few – when I knew that the singer and I were one: singing and playing with one voice, one heart and one mind. The accompanist is ever seeking this thrill. With no singer did I feel this more keenly or more often than when playing for Kathleen Ferrier. It is not to be taken for granted that, having rehearsed Schumann's 'Frauen Liebe und Leben' twenty or a hundred times, each knows exactly what the other partner is going to do. Yes, the *tempi* are settled to the mutual satisfaction of both; each knows when a slight increase of tone is to be made here, a decrease there; a minute quickening now, now a slackening; this phrase to be taken in one sweep, that phrase to be punctuated; weight of tone carefully balanced, and so forth. All this is routine, but the human element remains. Despite all your earnest thought and carefully laid plans, you never perform the same thing twice in exactly the same way. Each partner sensitively anticipates this and responds instantly to the thought, the urge, the inspiration of the other. With Kathleen you felt what she was going to do just before she did it. But could any accompanist hope to match her fierce burning, her melting tenderness, her noble vision, her radiance, her lightness of touch?

     .   .   .   .   .   .

I first played for Kathleen at a little concert in Lewes, Sussex, about twelve years ago. Then she was shy, unsure of herself and, to some extent, *gauche*. Apparently I had travelled down on the same train as she, but she had been too timid to come and speak; she peeped out of her carriage window on arrival, waited until I had alighted and then followed me at a distance. After the concert I told her how greatly I had been impressed by her, and I recall with some amusement that she asked me to give Roy Henderson a good report of her singing and to put in a good word for her with the concert agents and to the B.B.C. She did not know in those days how to present herself, how to walk on and off the platform, how to acknowledge her applause. I like to recall those early days and contrast them with her later triumphant progression through America, Germany, Italy, Holland, Scandinavia, France, and her own country. I think of the shouting and stamping of the huge audience at her last concert in Paris, of the capitulation of her packed audience in Cologne, of her last recital at the Royal Festival Hall, London. It was after this recital that Lord Esher said: 'I have today seen the two most remarkable women in England, the Queen and Kathleen Ferrier'.

As I have said, she had the poise to stand up to it all. More than that, she had wisdom. And she needed it, for societies the world over were clamouring for her services, knowing that their largest halls would be packed by a Ferrier recital. She could have sung seven afternoons and seven nights a week if she had accepted all the tempting engagements offered her. But that was not her style. She felt, in her wisdom, that it would cheapen her art to go careering about the world in an undignified way, getting in as many concerts or making as much money as she could. She was commanding higher fees than any singer here, and it was her responsibility to appear before those who engaged her vocally fresh, unfatigued by travel and toil. Every time Kathleen sang it was an event.

.   .   .   .   .   .

The news that she was mortally stricken was like a stab in the heart to us all. She not only bore her affliction with fortitude, she bore it with cheerfulness. At her bedside the conversation was of everything but herself; she would want to know what was happening in the world, and if you asked her how she was feeling, she would reply in that soft, vibrant voice: 'Don't let's go into that, luv, it's too boring. I'm feeling fine.' After communing with that indomitable spirit, the visitor came away cheered and fortified.

We last saw her not very long before the end, and looking anxiously at her we saw tiredness in her eyes. After a short stay, I suggested that as her *masseuse* was coming in half an hour it might be wise for her to rest. With ineffable sweetness she dismissed us with 'Eine kleine Pause'. We kissed and parted from one whose career had dazzled the world and been so tragically cut short.

There is no one who can throw a clearer light on this last period than Bernadine Hammond. She told me, to quote her own words, that 'morning after morning we went off to the hospital, and Kath would think of something interesting to do on the way home. We would stop at an antique shop and look at some glass; she would handle things with such love and say, "That does give me pleasure." She loved wood, and many are the tables and chairs she stroked. We would go in search of curtain material (Kath would always know exactly what she wanted), or some new kitchen utensil, or a gardening book she had seen advertised. There was much combined pleasure in the planning of meals, for Kath always maintained that eating was a great art. I remember one dreary day coming home in the taxi and Kath suddenly saying, "I know, I'll make an apple pie!". Instantly the fog vanished and we were soon eating boiling-hot apple pie.

'One of the amazing things about her was her complete acceptance of whatever came her way. If it was something good, then it was added to her mental list of blessings to be ever thankful for. This was an enormous help to her. At times when it seemed that she had more than any normal human could be expected to cope with, there would suddenly be that quick smile and there she was counting over what yet remained to her, and feeling sorry for people she considered worse off than herself. She hardly ever complained; on such rare occasions as she did, a saint would have done the same. She was her own greatest, most valiant helper, and never once did she let herself down. Any difficulty she looked upon in the light of a challenge and anything trying she said would pass in time.

'Kath enjoyed life from the moment she woke and purred over her morning cup of tea till I had removed Rosie the cat from under her bed at night. During the day she would say so often, "Lucky, lucky, Kath!". Troubles, and they were not infrequent, were never made much of. If there was anything she could do about it, then she did it smartly, otherwise she waited for it to blow over and turned her mind to something else. She used to say that the value of an illness was that it taught one to draw the dividing line between what mattered and what was of no consequence; she had a wonderful sense of proportion.

'She was an ordinary person and an extraordinary one. At first I was puzzled when I saw her on the concert platform, and I used to wonder how this woman, with her divine voice and lovely appearance, could possibly be the same as the one who spent the morning digging in the garden, and had been so excited to find parsley had come up that we had to have an omelette for lunch to do it justice. It suddenly occurred to me that that intrinsic loveliness was present in varying degrees in every single thing that she did. She once said that the Brahms' Serious Songs were the best sermon that she knew, and because she herself lived by that creed her singing of them was so deeply moving.'

Yes, Kathleen did regard these songs as a sermon. Wherever she gave a recital, in the sacred precincts of Peterborough or Southwark Cathedrals, or St Sepulchres in the City of London, she loved to sing 'The Four Serious Songs'.

Dr Bruno Walter says that 'it was particularly music of spiritual meaning that seemed Kathleen's most personal domain'. The truth of this was made increasingly evident in her last few years, when she loved to sing with me in private Schubert's 'Litanei' for All Souls' Day; 'Wanderers Nachtlied' (Wanderers' Nightsong), with its 'Warte nur, balde, ruhest du auch' (Only wait, you will find peace); and 'Die Allmacht', that mighty hymn of praise. I talked about the songs of Hugo Wolf to her, and here again, interesting to recall, it was his sacred songs which chiefly aroused her interest. From his Spanisches Liederbuch were three songs which moved her profoundly, they were 'Herr, was trägt der Boden hier, den du tränkst so bitterlich?' (Lord, what doth the soil bear here, which thou waterest with thy tears?); 'Nun wandre, Maria' (this is really a man's song, since it represents Joseph comforting Mary as they journey to Bethlehem before the birth of Jesus, but which Kathleen sang so beautifully); and 'Die ihr schwebet um diese Palmen' (Mary is fearful that the rustling of the palm trees in the wind will disturb the sleeping Child). The poem of this last has also been set by Brahms and recorded by Kathleen. And then Mörike's verse 'Auf ein altes Bild' was perhaps her favourite Wolf song (You are gazing on an old picture and see little Jesus playing on his Mother's knee; in the background a tree is growing, it is the tree from which the Cross will be made).

Kathleen did not study these songs but sang them for her own pleasure. I think now, in retrospect, though I did not realize it then, that there was some special reason for her doing this.

I remember once in Cologne suggesting that we visit the Dom. No sooner were we inside than Kathleen said she would like to sit; she asked me to walk around by myself. Thinking she was tired, I recommended returning immediately to the hotel, but 'No. I am not tired. I just want to sit and think!'.

Kathleen was not a person of whims and fancies, and I believe the reason for all this was that she was already aware, while admitting it to no one, that the sands of her life were running fast. I believe that her predilection for music of spiritual significance, for moments of quiet contemplation were natural reactions. Perhaps she gained strength and comfort and philosophy in this way.

On her last stay with us in the country when we suspected she was enduring some pain, she stood for a long time by herself at the end of the garden drinking in the view over Surrey and Sussex. It was suggested to Bernie that we should join her, but Bernie begged us not to disturb her as she loved to look, to listen, to think.

It was after this visit that she wrote us 'I am sitting up in bed, counting my blessings'.

.   .   .   .   .   .

In 1943 she was unknown. And less than ten years later Her Majesty the Queen was graciously pleased to decorate her as Commander of the British Empire. Ten years ago she was unknown. And last summer the Royal Philharmonic Society presented her with the highest award in music that this country can bestow – their Gold Medal – for her distinguished services to music.

And then – in the early summer of her glorious course – she left us. She left us for ever in her debt, for ever grateful for her example of nobility and humility, for her shining beauty and grace, for her goodness and her truth.

FAREWELL

by

Bruno Walter

It was in May 1952 that I saw Kathleen Ferrier for the last time. She sang with me Mahler's *Song of the Earth* in a Philharmonic Concert at Vienna's Grosser Musik-vereins-Saal; on the following days the London Decca Company recorded this work with us at the same place, and thereafter we left Vienna in the same plane. The last words and notes I heard her sing were those of the closing part of Mahler's work the 'Farewell' (Der Abschied). She stood at my side in all her beauty and vitality – and yet I remember to have felt in her singing of this farewell an ominous meaning. For with all her seemingly indefatigable freshness of singing during that long and tiring recording session, with all her power of expression, her enthusiasm and intense devotion, there was an overtone of finality in voice and emotion, there was a strange radiance in her eyes that made her performance – within the ideal render-ing of Mahler's work – a poignant, personal message.

Since then I cannot think of Mahler's *Song of the Earth* without seeing Kathleen Ferrier before me, without hearing the incomparably beautiful sound of her voice, visualizing the solemn transfiguration in her expression. She and this symphony of farewell – for not only the last song but the whole work has the meaning of a farewell – for ever they will belong together for me.

.   .   .   .   .   .

What tragic similarity of destinies is here revealed! It was in the shadow of death that Mahler conceived and wrote his *Song of the Earth* – and Kathleen Ferrier was approaching the same dark region when she sang it at that time in Vienna. In the different songs of his composition and with the words of Chinese poets Mahler takes his leave from grief and joy, from despair and love of our earthly life, until in the last one his soul unfolds its wings and – from afar already – greets the vanishing 'beloved earth'. Kathleen's expression in that performance was infinitely more than an ideal fulfilment of the composer's intentions – all the chords of her soul sounded and resounded with the sublime harmonies of that message from a kindred soul, and so what she sang became – perhaps unconsciously – her own farewell.

My acquaintance with Kathleen Ferrier began in 1946 in London. There I discussed with Rudolf Bing my programmes for the first season of the Edinburgh Festival in 1947. When I told him of my wish to perform Mahler's *Song of the Earth* and stressed the difficulty of finding singers who were qualified in voice and expression for the unusual demands of the work – and in particular of the parts for the alto – he said: 'There is a young singer of whom everybody speaks highly. Let me ask her to sing for you – perhaps you will find in her what you are looking for.'

So I met Kathleen in the house of friends of mine; and how well I remember that hour! She came in, not shy and not bold, but in modest self-confidence, dressed in a kind of Salzburg costume, a so-called 'dirndl', looking young and lovely, pure and earnest, simple and noble, and the room seemed to become brighter from the charm of her presence.

I asked her to sing *Lieder* by Brahms and, I believe, by Schubert; after these I begged her to try also some lines of *Song of the Earth*, which she did not know. She overcame their great difficulties with the ease of the born musician, and I recognized with delight that here was potentially one of the great singers of our time: a voice of a rare beauty, a natural production of tone, a genuine warmth of expression, an innate understanding of the musical phrase – a personality.

From this hour began a musical association which resulted in some of the happiest experiences of my life as a musician. Every time we met I found her grown in artistic stature and ripening into maturity, gaining control more and more of her wonderful gifts; the bud was breaking out into full bloom. At the same time our personal relationship became as close a friendship as the far too rare opportunities of our musical co-operation would permit. But my personal memories of those occasions, deep and indelible as they live on in me, are deplorably limited, and so, to my regret, this attempt to speak about Kathleen Ferrier cannot be sufficiently enlivened by characteristic personal details.

.   .   .   .

Yet, despite the rarity of the occasions when we saw each other, I feel as if I had known her through all my life. For she was – with all her depth and earnestness – very simple and natural; one could seem to read her mind like an open book, but only her singing revealed the abundant wealth of her inner life. Kathleen was born to sing, it was her individual way of self-expression; to hear her meant to feel her innermost affectionate, rich and lofty self. She was not enigmatic, not problematic, but a rare combination of profundity and clarity, of abundance and simplicity. Her uncomplicated mind had the intuitive understanding of the full variety of human emotions, and she could express them in her art with persuasive intensity.

She had the charm of a child and the dignity of a lady, or, to say it more drastically and perhaps more to the point, she was a country lass and also a priestess. When she sang an English folk-song – gay or sad – it had the natural, the authentic ring which revealed her as a child of the people; and just as convincing and authentic was her rendering of Bach's *St Matthew Passion* or Handel's *Messiah*. She loved fun like a child, and all kinds of innocent jokes, but in her relation to her art she had the humility and the inspiration of the initiate. No summit of solemnity was inaccessible to her, and it was particularly music of spiritual meaning that seemed her most personal domain.

.   .   .   .   .   .

I never had any discussion with Kathleen about religion, and so I do not know whether in that particular expressive power in her interpretation of works by Bach and Handel spoke a deep faith or only her intuitive artistic under-standing of the innermost meaning of their music. But this much I can say: when she sang religious works of this kind we heard more than the performance of a highly gifted artist, more than a congenial interpretation of a composer's work or of the words she sang; there spoke an inspiration which could only come from a deeper source than interpretative talent, and I am sure that in a longer life than that granted to her it would have become a dominant force in her soul.

As I said, I have only very few personal memories of Kathleen. But one I shall always cherish is that of our first piano rehearsals of Mahler's *Song of the Earth* in London. We always had to interrupt the last part of the 'Farewell' – she could not continue because her emotions overwhelmed her. Tears streamed down her cheeks; with all her will-power and vigour she could not help it, and only by and by did she learn to control her feelings. But nothing could be further from her than sentimentality – in those tears spoke strength of feeling, not weakness, and a deep comprehen-sion for another great heart.

.   .   .   .   .   .

Characteristic of her own heart, of its enchanting sim-plicity and loving-kindness, may be another memory. On her tour through the United States Kathleen had concerts in or near Los Angeles, but unfortunately it was at a time when my own activities kept me in New York. In order to make her sojourn in California as pleasant as possible, my daughter and I invited her to live in our house in Beverly Hills during the eight or ten days of her stay. When we came home after she had left, our faithful domestic helpers, a married Austrian couple, told us that Kathleen, on her free evenings, used to call them to the music-room, where she sat down at the piano, shed her shoes, and sang for them – to her heart's desire and, of course, to their utter delight. And just as no success and world fame could affect the friendly simplicity and modesty of this girl from Lancashire, so she remained as natural and sure of herself and of her dignity in her relation to 'society'.

.   .   .   .   .   .

So she was in art and in life a shining example, and whoever listened to her or met her personally felt enriched and uplifted. By her sublime art and by her loving nature she gave happiness and received happiness, and therefore no dirge shall be intoned to deplore her terrible suffering and early death – I know she herself would prefer to be remembered and spoken of in a major key.

Despite all my efforts to see her during the last time of her life, I was not given the opportunity – I could only send her messages of friendship and love and receive through friends her affectionate answers. We had said good-bye to each other at the airport in Zurich, where I left the plane that carried her on to London. I shall always see her as she stood there before me, the very image of courage and serenity, and I always shall hear her say, as she said whenever we parted, 'God bless you'. For the rest of my life I shall return these words, and think of her with the wish – God bless you, Kathleen!

The Royal Philharmonic Society's Gold Medal

Amongst the contributors to this book I am perhaps the only one who can write about the late Kathleen Ferrier in a strictly objective way, because socially I was nothing more than a passing acquaintance. I met her in all on five isolated occasions: once as a professional colleague in a performance of *Messiah* in a Lancashire town, the name of which I have forgotten, and on four other occasions in the company of friends.

I recall also how the Royal Philharmonic Society, by a swift and inspired action (yes, inspired is the word) was able to honour the greatest singer of our era at the eleventh hour of her life upon earth.

In the minutes of the proceedings of a meeting of the Honorary Committee of Management held on Friday, 8 May 1953, the following item occurs:

> '*Gold Medal.* In accordance with Bye-law 24 (*a*), it was proposed by Mr George Baker, seconded by Dr Allt, and unanimously agreed that it be recommended to the Annual General Meeting on 11 June that Miss Kathleen Ferrier be awarded the Gold Medal.
>
> The Secretary was instructed to circulate this additional item to the Agenda to all members, and to take all necessary preliminary steps.'

Behind this somewhat dry and official statement lies a very moving story.

I called one day upon Mrs Emmie Tillett, of Ibbs & Tillett,

to discuss some Philharmonic Society business, and at the end of our talk, when chatting about personal matters – Mrs Tillett and I are old and intimate friends – Emmie suddenly said: 'I suppose you know, George, that Kathleen is desperately ill, and I'm afraid there is no hope of recovery. Do you think the Phil could do anything?' I looked at her for a moment and then said, 'Do you mean the Gold Medal?' She nodded.

Involuntarily we both put out our hands to each other and gripped them. I said (and this is true): 'Emmie, the idea has been haunting me for weeks, and now this is the hour. I'll make the proposition at the next Committee meeting and, if need be, fight for it.'

I didn't have to fight for it; the members of the Committee supported me and, as our rules required, unanimously. Kathleen had won the fight, and the triumph was hers.

The Committee's decision required to be ratified by a General Meeting of the Society, and when the proposition was put before the Annual Meeting on 11 June 1953 that Kathleen Ferrier should be given the Gold Medal of the Royal Philharmonic Society, it was not only passed unanimously but there were many expressions of opinion about the justice and absolute rightness of the Committee's proposition, coupled with strange and almost eerie half-expressed emotional feelings that if it were possible the medal should be flown to her on wings. Such was the sense of impending doom.

Even mundane affairs like Annual Meetings can be charged with drama, and the meeting on 11 June 1953 was supercharged with both drama and an inexpressible depth of emotion.

So confident were David Ritson-Smith (the Honorary Secretary of the Society) and I that we would have the overwhelming support of the Annual Meeting that we gave an immediate order after the Committee Meeting on the 8 May for the medal to be struck, and so by 11 June it was ready for presentation. Our next problem was to find out when we could visit the hospital to make the presentation. Days passed, and then at last David Ritson-Smith went to the hospital alone on 20 June but, alas, Kathleen was too ill to see him.

However, I had fortunately written the following letter to Kathleen on 5 June:

MY DEAR KATHLEEN FERRIER,

All the members of the Royal Philharmonic Society send you their most affectionate greetings and would like you to know that the Committee of Management have unanimously decided to offer you the award of the Gold Medal of the Society for your distinguished services to music.

This decision of the Committee will receive the official sanction of the Annual General Meeting of the Royal Philharmonic Society on Thursday, 11 June, but in the meantime we would like you to know the sentiments of our hearts and the thoughts in our minds.

In due course – and soon – we will seek an opportunity to call upon you in order to present the medal on behalf of the Society.

We are, my dear Miss Ferrier,

Yours most sincerely,

GEORGE BAKER,

Chairman

DAVID RITSON-SMITH,

Honorary Secretary.

And here is her gracious and brave reply:

DEAR MR BAKER,

Thank you so very much for your most wonderful letter of 5 June.

Would you accept and convey to the Committee of Management my humble and deeply grateful thanks for offering me the award of the Gold Medal of the Royal Philharmonic Society. I accept with a very full heart and a real knowledge of the supreme honour you do me.

I am in hospital again and am, as yet, not allowed to see anyone – or have any knowledge of when I might be released from here. Mrs Tillett receives a regular bulletin and, as the telephone has been removed from my room, might I ask you if you could possibly contact her?

Your letter, with its unbelievable, wondrous news, has done more than anything to make me feel so much better. I have no words to describe my feelings on receiving it, but I send you all my affectionate greetings too, and renewed, sincere thanks from a very full heart.

Yours, in all sincerity,

KATHLEEN FERRIER.

I think it is appropriate to say that one of the proud privileges of the Royal Philharmonic Society is that for many long years – since 1871, to be precise – it has awarded a gold medal to the greatest contemporary musicians, both creative and executive. The list of the recipients is far too long to quote in full, but it includes such names as Gounod, Santley, Brahms, Paderewski, Kreisler, Kirkby Lunn, Casals, Henry Wood, Delius, Elgar, Beecham, Vaughan Williams, Bax, Rachmaninoff, Sibelius Strauss, Toscanini, Prokofiev, Walton, and Barbirolli. The mere recital of these few names will enable the reader to put the honour bestowed upon Kathleen Ferrier in its proper perspective.

The Gold Medal of the Royal Philharmonic Society is, in fact, one of the most coveted honours in the world of music, since it is bestowed by musicians on musicians.

The medal, bearing Beethoven's effigy, has been given to comparatively few singers, and there is an interregnum of thirty-nine years between 1914, when Miss Muriel Foster received it, and 1953, when we bestowed the Gold Medal on our beloved Kathleen.

In making the award when we did, the Royal Philharmonic Society was impelled to do so, not only by the poignant urgency of the tragic circumstances but because we knew that Kathleen

Ferrier had already achieved in a meteoric career of twelve years heights of artistry unattainable by less gifted people in a proverbial lifetime of three score years and ten. She was indeed blessed by God, and from the depths of her generous heart she showered her blessings upon us.

Proficiscere Anima Christiana.

GEORGE BAKER.

Records made by KATHLEEN FERRIER
for the DECCA RECORD COMPANY

LONG–PLAYING 33⅓ R.P.M. RECORDS

Schumann: *Frauenliebe und Leben*, Op. 42
Brahms: *Vier Ernste Gesänge*, Op. 121
KATHLEEN FERRIER & JOHN NEWMARK (Piano)   LXT2556

Mahler: *Das Lied von der Erde*; 4th side – *Three Rückert Songs*
KATHLEEN FERRIER & JULIUS PATZAK (Tenor),
with the Vienna Philharmonic Orchestra,
conducted by BRUNO WALTER   LXT2721-2

Brahms: *Rhapsody for Contralto*, Male Chorus and Orchestra,
Op. 53
KATHLEEN FERRIER, with the London Philharmonic
Orchestra and Choir, conducted by CLEMENS KRAUSS

Four Songs
KATHLEEN FERRIER & PHYLLIS SPURR (Piano)   LXT2850

Decca translation booklets are available for the above three recordings,
giving the German words and an English prose translation.

A Broadcast Recital by Kathleen Ferrier (5 June 1952)
The Fairy Lough, Op. 77, No. 2 (Stanford); A Soft Day, Op. 141,
No. 3 (Stanford); Love is a bable, Op. 152, No. 3 (Parry); Silent
Noon (Vaughan Williams).
Go not, happy day (Bridge); Sleep (Warlock); Pretty Ring-time
(Warlock); O waly, waly (arr. Britten); Come you not from
Newcastle? (arr. Britten); Kitty, my love (arr. Hughes).
KATHLEEN FERRIER with FREDERICK STONE (Piano)
                                                     LX3133

Gluck: *Orfeo* (*Orpheus and Euridice*) (an abridged version of the
  Glyndebourne production)

  Cast:

  Orfeo   ..   ..   KATHLEEN FERRIER
  Euridice   ..   ..   ANN AYARS (Soprano)
  Amore   ..   ..   ZOE VLACHOPOULOS (Soprano)

  with the Glyndebourne Festival Chorus and the Southern
  Philharmonic Orchestra, conducted by Fritz Stiedry

  LXT2893

A Recital of Bach arias; A Recital of Handel arias

  KATHLEEN FERRIER (Contralto) with the London Philharmonic Orchestra, conducted by SIR ADRIAN BOULT

  LXT2757

Bach: Cantata No. 11 – Praise our God   LX3006
  Cantata No. 67 – Hold in affection Jesus Christ *and*
  Jesu, joy of man's desiring   LX3007

  KATHLEEN FERRIER, WILLIAM HERBERT (Tenor), WILLIAM
  PARSONS (Bass) and, on LX3006 only, ENA MITCHELL
  (Soprano) with the Cantata Singers and the Jacques
  Orchestra, conducted by DR REGINALD JACQUES

Folk and Traditional Songs

  KATHLEEN FERRIER & PHYLLIS SPURR (Piano)   LX3040

Songs of the British Isles

  KATHLEEN FERRIER & PHYLLIS SPURR (Piano)   LX3098

MEDIUM-PLAYING 33⅓ R.P.M. RECORDS

A Recital of Arias

  Handel: *Serse* – Ombra mai fu
  Rodelinde – Art thou troubled?

  Gluck: *Orfeo* – What is life?

  KATHLEEN FERRIER, with the London Symphony
  Orchestra, conducted by SIR MALCOLM SARGENT

  Mendelssohn: *Elijah*—O rest in the Lord

  KATHLEEN FERRIER

  with the Boyd Neel Orchestra, conducted by BOYD NEEL

  LW5072

Handel: *Messiah* – O thou that tellest; He was despised
        Samson – Return, O God of hosts
        Judas Maccabaeus – Father of Heaven
        KATHLEEN FERRIER
        with the London Symphony Orchestra, conducted by
        SIR ADRIAN BOULT   LW5076

Bach: *St Matthew Passion* – Grief for Sin
     St John Passion – All is fulfilled
     Mass in B Minor – Qui sedes; Agnus Dei
     KATHLEEN FERRIER
     with the London Philharmonic Orchestra, conducted by
     SIR ADRIAN BOULT   LW5083

Mahler: Three Rückert Songs
     KATHLEEN FERRIER
     with the Vienna Philharmonic Orchestra, conducted by
     BRUNO WALTER   LW5123

Schumann: *Frauenliebe und Leben*, Op. 42
     KATHLEEN FERRIER with JOHN NEWMARK (Piano) LW5089
     Volksliedchen, Op. 51, No. 2; *Widmung*, Op. 25, No. 1
     KATHLEEN FERRIER with PHYLLIS SPURR (Piano) LW5098

Brahms: *Four Serious Songs*, Op. 121 (Vier ernste Gesänge)
     KATHLEEN FERRIER with JOHN NEWMARK (Piano) LW5094

Schubert: *Gretchen am Spinnrade*, Op. 2; *Die junge Nonne*, Op. 43,
     No. 1; *An die Musik*, Op. 88, No. 4; *Der Musensohn*,
     Op. 92, No. 1
     KATHLEEN FERRIER with PHYLLIS SPURR (Piano) LW5098

78 R.P.M. RECORDS

Handel: Art thou troubled?
Gluck: What is life?
     KATHLEEN FERRIER, with the London Symphony
     Orchestra, conducted by SIR MALCOLM SARGENT   K1466

Pergolesi: *Stabat Mater*
     JOAN TAYLOR (Soprano), KATHLEEN FERRIER, and the
     Nottingham Oriana Choir with the Boyd Neel String
     Orchestra, conducted by ROY HENDERSON   AK1517-21

Mendelssohn: O rest in the Lord; Woe unto them
> KATHLEEN FERRIER, with the Boyd Neel String Orchestra,
> conducted by BOYD NEEL   K1556

Schubert: *Gretchen am Spinnrade; Die junge Nonne*
> KATHLEEN FERRIER and PHYLLIS SPURR (Piano)   K1632

Gluck: *Orfeo* – a concise version of the Glyndebourne production
> KATHLEEN FERRIER, ZOE VLACHOPOULOS (Soprano), and
> ANN AYARS (Soprano), with the Glyndebourne Festival
> Chorus, and the Southern Philharmonic Orchestra,
> conducted by FRITZ STIEDRY   AK1656-62

J. S. Bach: *St Matthew Passion*
> ELSIE SUDDABY (Soprano), KATHLEEN FERRIER, ERIC
> GREENE (Tenor), BRUCE BOYCE (Bass), GORDON CLINTON
> (Bass), HENRY CUMMINGS (Bass) and WILLIAM PARSONS
> (Bass), with the Bach Choir and the Jacques Orchestra,
> conducted by DR REGINALD JACQUES   AK2001-21

> *St Matthew Passion* – Excerpts
> ELSIE SUDDABY (Soprano), KATHLEEN FERRIER, ERIC
> GREENE (Tenor), BRUCE BOYCE (Bass), and WILLIAM
> PARSONS (Bass), with the Bach Choir and the Jacques
> Orchestra, conducted by DR REGINALD JACQUES K1673-9

(For full details of these Bach records, please see pp. 176-8 of the
Decca 78 r.p.m. catalogue of March 1951.)

Handel: Ombra mai fu
> KATHLEEN FERRIER, with the London Symphony
> Orchestra, conducted by SIR MALCOLM SARGENT
>   one side of K2135

Brahms: *Vier ernste Gesänge*, Op. 121
> KATHLEEN FERRIER and JOHN NEWMARK (Piano)
>   AX563-4

Rhapsody for Contralto, Male Chorus and Orchestra,
Op. 53
> KATHLEEN FERRIER, with the London Philharmonic
> Orchestra and Choir, conducted by CLEMENS KRAUSS
>   AK1847-8

78 R.P.M. RECORDS – *continued*

Brahms: Two Songs for Contralto with Viola Obbligato, Op. 91
KATHLEEN FERRIER with PHYLLIS SPURR (Piano) and MAX
GILBERT (Viola)   K2289

Schubert: *An die Musik,* Op. 88, No. 4; *Der Musensohn,* Op. 92,
No. 1
KATHLEEN FERRIER and PHYLLIS SPURR (Piano)   M652

Miscellaneous: Silent night, holy night; Adeste Fideles
KATHLEEN FERRIER, with the Boyd Neel String Orchestra,
conducted by BOYD NEEL   M622

The Fidgety Bairn; Ca' the yowes
KATHLEEN FERRIER and JOHN NEWMARK (Piano)   M657

Ye banks and braes; Drink to me only with thine eyes
KATHLEEN FERRIER and PHYLLIS SPURR (Piano)   M679

Now sleeps the crimson petal; To daisies
KATHLEEN FERRIER and PHYLLIS SPURR (Piano)   M680

I know where I'm going; I will walk with my love;
The stuttering lovers
KATHLEEN FERRIER and PHYLLIS SPURR (Piano)   M681

Blow the wind southerly; Ma bonny lad; The keel row
KATHLEEN FERRIER and PHYLLIS SPURR (Piano)   F9300

Records made by KATHLEEN FERRIER
for the COLUMBIA GRAPHOPHONE COMPANY

LONG–PLAYING 33⅓ R.P.M. RECORD
Mahler: *Kindertotenlieder*
KATHLEEN FERRIER, with the Vienna Philharmonic
Orchestra, conducted by BRUNO WALTER   33C1009

78 R.P.M. RECORDS

Handel: *Otone*—Spring is Coming; Come to me, Soothing Sleep
KATHLEEN FERRIER with GERALD MOORE (Piano) DX1194

Handel: *Otone*—I will lay me down in peace; O praise the Lord
KATHLEEN FERRIER with GERALD MOORE (Piano) DB2152*

Mahler: *Kindertotenlieder*
KATHLEEN FERRIER, with the Vienna Philharmonic
Orchestra, conducted by BRUNO WALTER   LX8939-41

Mendelssohn: I would that my love; Greeting
Duets—KATHLEEN FERRIER and ISOBEL BAILLIE (Soprano)
with GERALD MOORE (Piano)   DB2194

Purcell: Sound the trumpet; Let us wander; Shepherd, shepherd
KATHLEEN FERRIER with GERALD MOORE (Piano) DB2201*

* These records are now deleted from the Columbia catalogue, and,
as far as is known, it is not planned to reissue them.

It is tragic that no recording exists of Kathleen Ferrier's singing of
the Angel in *The Dream of Gerontius.*